30-MINUTE GROUPS

ANXIETY MANAGEMENT

CALMING THE MIND, CHALLENGING THOUGHTS, AND BUILDING CONFIDENCE

DR. LEiGH BAGWELL

Duplication and Copyright

No part of this publication may be reproduced, stored in a retrieval system, or transmitted in any form by any means, electronic, mechanical, photocopy, video or audio recording, or otherwise without prior written permission from the publisher, except for all worksheets and activities which may be reproduced for a specific group or class. Reproduction for an entire school or school district is prohibited.

NCYI titles may be purchased in bulk at special discounts for educational, business, fundraising, or promotional use. For more information, please email sales@ncyi.org.

P.O. Box 22185
Chattanooga, TN 37422-2185
423.899.5714 • 866.318.6294
fax: 423.899.4547 • www.ncyi.org

ISBN: 9781965066010
© 2024 National Center for Youth Issues, Chattanooga, TN
All rights reserved.
Written by: Dr. Leigh Bagwell
Published by National Center for Youth Issues
Printed in the U.S.A. • August 2025

Third party links are accurate at the time of publication, but may change over time.

The information in this book is designed to provide helpful information on the subjects discussed and is not intended to be used, nor should it be used, to diagnose or treat any mental health or medical condition. For diagnosis or treatment of any mental health or medical issue, consult a licensed counselor, psychologist, or physician. The publisher and author are not responsible for any specific mental or physical health needs that may require medical supervision, and are not liable for any damages or negative consequences from any treatment, action, application, or preparation, to any person reading or following the information in this book. References are provided for informational purposes only and do not constitute endorsement of any websites or other sources.

ASCA National Model®, Recognized ASCA Model Program® and RAMP® are registered trademarks of the American School Counselor Association. Our use of them does not imply an affiliation with or endorsement by the American School Counselor Association.

Contents

Introduction 4
   What's Included. 5
   Accompanying Group Documents 6

Introductory Group Session 8

Chapter 1: Is Anxiety Normal? 10

Chapter 2: Your Brain on Anxiety 16

Chapter 3: Your Body on Anxiety 23

Chapter 4: Types of Anxiety 30

Chapter 5: The Think-Feel-Do Cycle 37

Chapter 6: Interrupting the Think-Feel-Do Cycle 43

Chapter 7: Coping Skills – Mindfulness 50

Chapter 8: Coping Skills - Relaxation 57

Chapter 9: Coping Skills – Breathing 64

Chapter 10: Personal Anxiety Management Planning 71

Final Group Session 77

Small Group Action Planning Guide 79

Anxiety Management Group Permission Form 80

Anxiety Management Group Expectations 81

Group Attendance Form 82

Group Attendance Form (Example) 83

Pre- and Post- Group Survey 84

Pre- and Post- Group Survey Answer Key 86

Post-Group Survey Results 87

Post-Group Survey Results (Example) 88

Certificate of Completion 89

Anxiety Management Group Completion Letter 90

References 91

About The Author 92

A Brief Look at Leigh's Workshop Sessions 93

Also Available from Leigh 94

30-Minute Groups 95

About NCYI 96

Introduction

As a school counselor, school social worker, or school-based mental health professional, you may offer this group curriculum if there are multiple students experiencing anxiety. Small group counseling is a beneficial service as it lets students know that they are not alone in their experience and allows often-understaffed schools to serve more students with evidence-based practices.

In a world where rates of anxiety are increasing and trending younger, providing youth with the skills to understand and manage these emotions is a necessity. Giving children strategies to build a positive relationship with their emotional world and cope with big feelings will improve their self-concept and ripple out to other parts of their lives and interpersonal relationships.

This small group counseling curriculum consists of ten to twelve thirty-minute lessons to help students learn these necessary skills. Our goals with this curriculum are to:

- **Help students manage their anxiety, not fully eliminate it.** It is not realistic to think that all the stressors that cause anxiety can be removed. Instead, when students learn to manage their feelings and experiences, their anxiety should naturally decrease over time. So rather than try to avoid experiences and situations that may create anxiety, teach students effective strategies they can use when they feel anxiety.

- **Create space for students to share their feelings without judgment.** Listening is an important form of communication with students. Validate their experiences without minimizing or exaggerating them. Allowing students to hear others share similar feelings and experiences builds a network of support and understanding.

- **Empower and encourage the student to face their feelings and use their new skills to endure and overcome moments of anxiety.** Discuss students' situations and help them generate specific strategies for managing their feelings. Praise their efforts, even if they are not always successful. Give them opportunities to practice skills in a safe environment and provide actionable feedback. The support and encouragement they experience in the sessions often extend beyond the group.

This small group counseling curriculum can be used with elementary to middle school-aged students who are struggling with anxiety. Most of the lessons focus on general anxiety. However, some lessons focus on understanding specific types of anxiety as well. This group will focus on building skills related to understanding and normalizing anxiety, its connection to the brain and body, different types of anxiety, and, perhaps most importantly, strategies to manage anxiety when it occurs. This curriculum recognizes the unique ways in which each student learns, emphasizing that there is no singular 'correct' way to embrace these ideas.

The strategic design of these group sessions allows students to empathize, connect with others, and translate their new knowledge into practice. The American School Counselor Association (ASCA®)-aligned curriculum contains an introductory lesson, ten core anxiety management lessons, and a final closing lesson. Facilitators have the flexibility to include the initial and final lessons as part of the core lessons if they have extra time.

You will find a range of essential resources in the book's concluding pages. These consist of permission and completion letters, attendance logs, a group expectation form, and a Certificate of Completion.

You will also find Pre- and Post-Group Surveys to measure the success of the lessons and templates. You can use these to share the results with stakeholders. Moreover, this workbook provides a comprehensive small group action plan that will integrate effortlessly into your ASCA® evaluation document and facilitate a seamless transition from planning to assessment.

Practical and applicable, the activities provided are suitable for small groups and do not require additional materials. You do not need supplies beyond pencils, a whiteboard or chalkboard, markers or crayons, and scratch paper; you will not need to spend hours prepping materials before meeting with your students.

Everything you need is included!

See page 91 for information on Downloadable Resources.

What's Included?

Anxiety Management Group Lesson Plans: Comprises ten lessons and all necessary documents to conduct these small group sessions. Following the overview of the lesson curriculum, you will find supporting documentation to develop a small group within the school setting.

Mind Map: Provides an illustrated diagram of the skills and concepts related to the lesson. To help students make connections between what they are learning. Students should begin each lesson by considering the meaning of the specific skill. It is optional to write these, but visuals are helpful for many students. Some have found it helpful to draw the Mind Map on the board, or drawing a tree with the concept written on the trunk and the related words on the fruit on the tree.

ASCA® Standards: Each lesson includes success criteria for the learning target.

Lesson Introduction: At the start of each lesson, we will introduce a concept and explain it to provide clarity for the upcoming story.

Circle Time Questions: This section has three optional questions for the facilitator to start the conversation. These questions allow students to deepen their understanding of the topic and build community by discussing and sharing their experiences.

Story Time: Provides stories related to the topic that should be read aloud to help students understand the concept.

Coloring Sheets: Allow students to visualize the lesson topic. Students can color the sheet while the facilitator shares the initial story after the lesson is complete or take it home with them.

Discussion Questions: Students can discuss the questions posed to help them process their beliefs on the subject.

Skill Practice: Allow students to share how they would apply the concepts of the lesson, giving them each a chance to answer one question.

Additional Activities: Provides activities to help students practice and apply the lesson concept.

Closing Considerations: Provides an opportunity to review the concept and ask students to reflect on their new experience with the material.

Would You Rather? Game: Provides an opportunity for students to consider what they would "rather" do related to the lesson's topic. The facilitator can cut out the cards and let students discuss or read aloud while students move from one side of the room to the other to communicate their preferred answer.

Accompanying Group Documents

Small Group Action Plan Guide: Provides the necessary information required to complete the ASCA® National Model's Small Group Action Plan.

Permission Form: The permission form is used to gain the permission of the student's caregivers for the child to attend the Anxiety Management Group.

Group Expectations: Basic expectations for the group process. The form has space for the facilitator and group to collaborate on adding additional expectations to fit their group.

Group Attendance Form: This is a blank form that allows the facilitator to track which students attended each session and what topics were discussed.

Group Attendance Form (Example): This form is an example of how to best utilize the group attendance form.

Pre- and Post-Group Survey: Provides an opportunity for students to share what they know of the concepts before and after they have completed the curriculum.

To measure the progress of students who participate, use the same assessment for both the Pre-Group and Post-Group Survey. Administer the Pre-Group Survey during the first group session, before instruction and practice opportunities for new skills or knowledge.

At the end of the group sessions, administer the Post-Group Survey. Compare the results of both assessments to identify areas of knowledge and skills gained as well as areas that need further instruction. Then calculate the average score of the pre-survey and post-survey to determine the percentage of improvement by subtracting the pre-survey average from the post-assessment average and then dividing the result by the pre-survey average. Use this pre-survey average improvement to measure the students' progress effectively.

Percentage of Improvement Formula:
((Post-Group Total - Pre-Group Total) / Pre-Group Total)) x 100 = Percentage of Overall Improvement

Example:
((57 Post Group Total - 18 Pre-Group Total) / 18) x 100 = 216.6% Overall Improvement

Review school and student data to determine who should attend the group. This includes behavior referrals, attendance data, and achievement metrics to identify at-risk students. The impact of the small group intervention is demonstrated when strategically selecting students and closely monitoring their academic, attendance, and behavior data. Be sure to share the assessment of the intervention with your school counseling advisory council.

Post-Group Survey Results: The survey shows one way to share your data with your interested parties. Remember, we want to make sure that we use graphs and charts as they show our data, which is often more impactful than a paragraph of text. Use whatever platform you prefer to show your data but be sure to complete the data following the group and then share with your counseling program's stakeholders.

Post-Group Survey Results (Example): The survey shows what your data might resemble following the completion of the groups. You can use this form to share your data.

Certificate of Completion: Present students with a certificate to congratulate them on completing the curriculum.

Anxiety Management Group Completion Letter: Letter written to the caregivers of students that highlights the skills and knowledge addressed during the group. Provide students with their certificate and their Anxiety Management Group Completion letter during the last lesson.

Additional Materials: You will need to make copies of the pre- and Post-Group Survey surveys and print the Coloring Sheets for each participating student. You might also print and cut the "Would You Rather?" game or facilitate that activity verbally. Additionally, you might want to have a whiteboard or chalkboard accessible for group brainstorming. We recommend having crayons or colored pencils readily available on the table for those who wish to complete the coloring sheet. It might also be helpful to have some fidgets accessible for your students during their group session.

Good luck with your group! We hope you have a fantastic experience supporting your students with anxiety!

Introductory Group Session

Directions and Overview

Conducting this introductory session is recommended but not required, as the content covered here can easily integrate into the first core Anxiety Management Group lesson. Once you have identified students to participate in the group and confirmed they have permission from caregivers, determine the activities based on the students' needs.

Directions: We recommend that you meet with the students to complete this introductory group session before conducting the first core lesson. You will start by welcoming all the students to the group. Explain to the students that the purpose of the group is to:

- understand what is happening in our brains when we feel anxiety;
- learn to identify the things that trigger our anxiety so that we can work to prevent some of our anxiety; and
- learn coping skills to help us when we do feel anxiety.

Make sure to instill hope for gaining new knowledge and having fun together!

Survey: If administering a Pre-Group Survey, do as part of the first group session. It is not necessary to assess each group session. Instead, conduct assessments at the beginning and end of the group experience. Feel free to adapt or use your own assessments to meet your program needs. The questions in the Pre- and Post-Small Group Surveys are designed to test for both knowledge gained and how the students have applied the knowledge they learned in the group.

Depending on the grade level of the students in your group, you may select three to five questions from the Pre- and Post-Group Surveys instead of having them complete the full assessment. Choose questions that align with your goals for the group. Using the same questions for the Pre- and Post-Group Surveys is best practice and allows you to measure growth for each student. Additionally, you may present the questions in a manner appropriate for your students and group dynamics (paper, electronically, etc.).

Introductions: Help your students get to know one another by asking them to share their names, something about themselves, and what they hope to learn from the group. They can also share one unique fact about themselves. Feel free to adapt other creative introduction activities. For example, ask each student to introduce themselves as a superhero using their name and what superpower they would like to have. Remind students that all answers should be appropriate for school. As the group leader, be sure to participate as well. Explain that during each session, they will be asked to share a high and low for the week or check-in using the weather to represent their emotions. Offer to practice that check-in now.

Icebreaker Activity: Choose from one of the icebreaker activities below (or select one of your own). The activity should provide an opportunity for all students in the group to participate and learn more about each other, building a stronger group dynamic.

- **World's Worst**: Have each student choose a profession they think they would be the worst at doing. As students share with the group, brainstorm something the world's worst _____ would say. For example, the world's worst dentist might say, "Please take a bag of candy from the toy chest as you leave!"

- **Autobiography**: Have each person sum up their life in one sentence. They can also choose a movie, book, or song that reflects their autobiography.

Explain the Group Format: Review the group meeting schedule and procedures for attending (Will students report to the counseling office? Will they receive a pass on the day of the group? Etc.). Explain that, in each meeting, you will discuss the lesson topic, hear a student story, and then answer questions. Discuss the logistics of what they will do while you are reading; they will be eating (if it is a lunch group) or completing their Coloring Sheet. Explain that they will practice skills introduced in the lesson and play a "Would You Rather?" game. Finally, explain that at the end of each session, they will be asked to give a one-sentence overview of what they have learned and make a plan to practice that lesson topic throughout the week.

Review Group Expectations: Print a copy of the Anxiety Management Group Expectations. Review the expectations together with the students and answer questions as they arise. Ask the students what other conditions are important for everyone to feel safe and able to learn together. (Avoid using the word "rule" to prevent the experience from seeming punitive.) Take time to collaborate with your group to determine whether you need to modify or add expectations. Once the group has identified appropriate expectations, allow students to ask questions and then come to a consensus on the group norms.

Group Conclusion: Allow students to ask any final questions about the group. Ask each student to summarize the information they learned from this lesson into one sentence. Students may share with partners or the group. Remind students of the Group Norms, particularly about not repeating what was shared in the group, and the time and date of the next meeting. Be sure to thank them for their participation.

Note to Facilitators: You can customize the material to fit the needs of your group. If your students are not yet readers, you can read the "Would You Rather?" game questions aloud and request that students move to different sides of the room to show their answers. Students can write their responses to questions instead of sharing them aloud or break into smaller teams to discuss. Some facilitators may choose to incorporate traditional games into the lessons if they have longer session times. Remember, the workbook is just the framework, but you will bring it to life!

IS ANXIETY NORMAL?

MIND MAP

On the board, draw a mind map and ask students to consider the meaning of *Anxiety*.

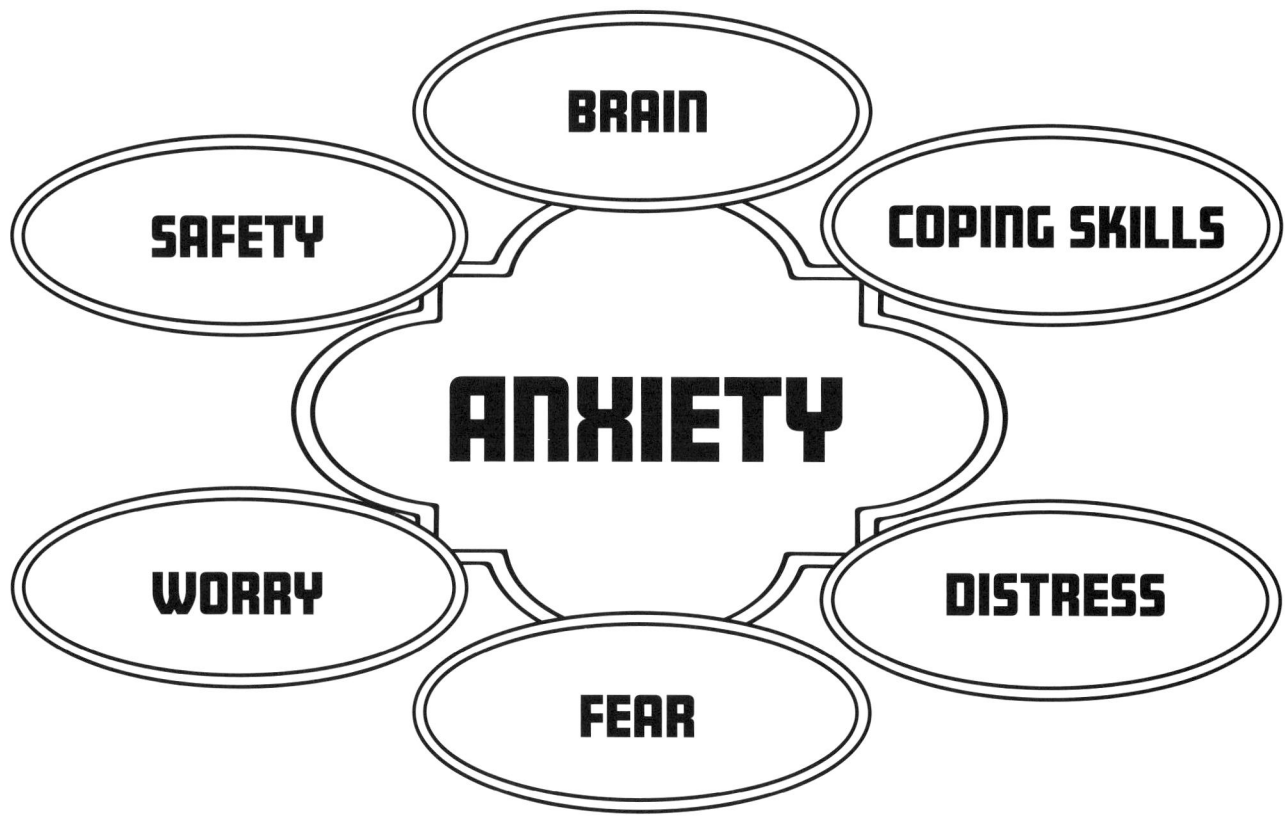

ASCA® STANDARDS

- **B-SMS 6.** Ability to identify and overcome barriers
- **B-SS 2.** Positive, respectful, and supportive relationships with students who are similar to and different from them
- **B-SS 3.** Positive relationships with adults to support success
- **B-SS 9.** Social maturity and behaviors appropriate to the situation and environment

DIRECTIONS

- Prior to the first group, be sure your students have completed the Pre-Group Survey. Complete a brief check-in with your students by asking them to share a high and low for the week or by using the weather to represent their emotions.
- Review the Group Expectations.
- Read the Lesson Introduction and ask the Circle Time Questions before reading the Story and asking the Discussion Questions. Students can work in pairs to craft their responses or share with the whole group.
- Complete the Skill Practice, "Would You Rather?" game, and Additional Activities as time allows.
- Be sure to complete the Closing Considerations with each session.

Definitions:

- **Anxiety** is the excessive concern about a potential triggering event or perceived threat to one's safety. That safety can be physical, emotional, or social.
- To **cope** is to deal appropriately with something difficult.

LESSON INTRODUCTION

Anxiety is a normal part of life. When we feel worried or nervous, it is our body's way of letting us know that we may not be safe or that we are getting ready to do something that we care a lot about.

However, when we feel high levels of worry that cause us physical and mental distress, these feelings can impact what we want or need to do. We may be experiencing what is considered a high level of anxiety that requires more support and intervention, which could include counseling and/or medical support.

Many people will experience high levels of anxiety sometime during their school-aged years. It is important to recognize these symptoms and learn skills that help us manage these feelings so we can cope during difficult times. It is also very important to know it is okay to have these feelings and to reach out to trusted adults for help and support when we feel overwhelmed.

CIRCLE TIME QUESTIONS

Ask students to reflect and share their answers to the following questions with the group.

- Can you think of a time in your life when you have experienced anxiety?
- When was a time you had difficulty coping?
- When was a time that you were able to cope successfully?

STORY TIME

Hand out coloring sheets and crayons or markers to younger students while the facilitator reads the story, if desired.

You are Not Alone

Donnell had always been a nervous person, but he was especially nervous on the first day at his new school. His mind fired off question after question. What if his new teachers were not nice? What if he did not like his classmates? What if he did not have a good view of the board from his seat? What if he did not find friends? In the past, he was able to get the answers to all his questions pretty quickly, but this year was different.

He had been in school for two months, but he was still so nervous every single day he almost did not want to go to school anymore. Every day it felt like there were 100 more unanswered questions that popped into his head, and some of them did not seem to have answers. I mean, how was anyone supposed to answer, "What if something bad happens tomorrow?" This had never happened to Donnell before, and it filled him with confusion (which made him worry more!). Everything just felt like it was too much. The worst part was that it did not seem like any of his classmates were nervous at all, which made him feel like there must be something different and wrong about him.

One afternoon, as Donnell was nervously trying to decide where to sit for lunch, another student came up to him. She seemed so confident; Donnell was getting nervous just looking at her.

"Hi, I'm Amelia. I'm new to this school. And honestly, I have no idea where to sit for lunch and it's got me so stressed. Maybe we can sit together?" she said.

Donnell could not believe his ears. She did not look stressed at all!

"Of course," Donnell stammered. "I am new too and was stressed about where to sit. Sometimes it's so hard to make a choice."

Amelia gave a wide smile.

"Right? Well, at least now we can help each other."

Donnell breathed a sigh of relief. He still had many unanswered questions, but at least he had the answer to one of them: *Am I the only stressed one in this school?* Even though he was still nervous, it was nice to know he was not alone.

DISCUSSION QUESTIONS

- Was Donnell having normal anxiety or high levels of anxiety? What evidence from the story supports your opinion?
- What was something that helped Donnell?
- What could Donnell have done that would have made his anxiety worse?
- What other ideas do you have that might help Donnell better cope in the future?

SKILL PRACTICE

Ask students how they might apply what Donnell learned about everyone having anxiety, giving every student a chance to answer one question. Skill practice can be adapted to allow students to answer in pairs or record their answers on the worksheet.

How might you (or someone else) cope with anxiety:

- When you think that you are the only one who is anxious?
- When you are in an uncomfortable situation with a person you know?
- When you are around strangers?
- When someone does something that upsets you?
- When you are not sure the reason you feel anxious?
- When your anxiety is unexpected?
- When it seems like the amount of anxiety you are feeling is bigger than is normal?

ADDITIONAL ACTIVITIES

- Break the students into pairs and have them take turns role-playing a person with symptoms of anxiety and a calm person. How can they tell when their role-play partner is anxious versus calm? Have them list the differences they notice. Each student should have the opportunity to role-play both dispositions.
- Have students think about the concept of, "You are not alone," specifically in the context of having anxiety. Give them the opportunity to reflect on the fact that having at least some anxiety is a universal experience. They can draw, journal, or talk with a partner about how it feels knowing that everyone experiences anxiety. If there is time, they can share.

CLOSING CONSIDERATIONS

Anxiety is a normal part of life, and if we are not able to cope effectively, it can get in the way. It is important to understand that even if you do have bigger anxiety than others, you are not alone. It is also important to take steps to help yourself manage your anxiety and cope with stress.

Ask students to summarize the content of the lesson in one sentence. Students may share their answers either with a partner or the whole group. Ask students to notice times this week when they observe someone else being anxious or if they feel anxious themselves.

"WOULD YOU RATHER?" GAME

Playing the "Would You Rather?" game is a fun and engaging activity for students to develop their critical thinking skills. Students will reflect on their experience, evaluate their options based on their preferences, and reflect on the opinions of others, providing a different perspective and strengthening their sense of connection to one another.

WOULD YOU RATHER?

Copy and cut out the questions for small groups to discuss, or have students stand in the center of the room and move towards one side or the other to show their vote for either option as the facilitator reads the questions aloud.

- WOULD YOU RATHER GO TO A NEW SCHOOL OR STAY IN THE SAME SCHOOL?
- WOULD YOU RATHER TRY A NEW HOBBY OR KEEP THE SAME HOBBY?
- WOULD YOU RATHER ASK QUESTIONS OR KEEP YOUR QUESTIONS TO YOURSELF?
- WOULD YOU RATHER TELL SOMEONE YOU ARE STRESSED OR WAIT FOR SOMEONE TO ASK?
- WOULD YOU RATHER KEEP YOUR WORRIES TO YOURSELF OR WRITE THEM DOWN?
- WOULD YOU RATHER FEEL ALONE OR FEEL LIKE YOU HAVE SUPPORT?

30-MINUTE GROUPS: **ANXIETY MANAGEMENT**

YOUR BRAIN ON ANXIETY

MIND MAP

On the board, draw a mind map and ask students to consider the meaning of *Feeling Brain*.

ASCA® STANDARDS

- **B-SMS 6.** Ability to identify and overcome barriers
- **B-SMS 1.** Responsibility for self and actions
- **B-SMS 10.** Ability to manage transitions and adapt to change

DIRECTIONS

- Complete a brief check-in with your students by asking them to share a high and low for the week or by using the weather to represent their emotions.
- Review the Group Expectations.
- Read the Lesson Introduction and ask the Circle Time Questions before reading the Story and asking the Discussion Questions. Students can work in pairs to craft their responses or share with the whole group.
- Complete the Skill Practice, "Would You Rather?" game, and Additional Activities as time allows.
- Be sure to complete the Closing Considerations with each session.

Definitions:

- The **Amygdala**, or the Feeling Brain, is the part of the brain responsible for processing emotions.
- The **Fight, Flight, Freeze, or Fawn response** is the physiological response our brains have to acute stress that signals our body that we are in danger.

LESSON INTRODUCTION

Anxiety is a physiological response to a perceived threat in the environment. That response prepares the body to quickly protect itself from danger. The brain notices a trigger and determines whether it is threat. When the amygdala (the part of the brain responsible for processing emotions) reacts to the threat, it activates the sympathetic nervous system by releasing hormones that include adrenaline and noradrenaline.

There are four ways the body responds to that release of hormones and the amygdala's call for protection:

- **Fight:** face the danger and fight the threat aggressively.
- **Flight:** run away from the threat to try and save yourself.
- **Freeze:** do not move or hide in hopes of being ignored until the threat passes.
- **Fawn:** submit to or bargain with the threat in hopes of avoiding conflict.

The Fight, Flight, Freeze, Fawn response can happen in the face of imminent physical danger or of psychological threats, real threats or imaginary ones. There are also times when, if a threat continues for an extended period, you may experience more than one response

The amygdala functions unconsciously and almost instantaneously, but that does not mean that it is always accurate. For people under acute stress or with high levels anxiety, the sympathetic nervous system is always on guard. Therefore, the amygdala is hypersensitive and will react to things that others would not recognize as threatening.

However, if we can interrupt the process before the amygdala takes over, we can think through the situation and evaluate whether it truly is a threat or not. If we recognize when our bodies are starting to react to feelings of anxiety, we can interrupt the Fight, Flight, Freeze, Fawn response by using appropriate coping skills to reduce the anxiety we feel.

CIRCLE TIME QUESTIONS

Ask students to reflect and share their answers to the following questions with the group.

- When you are feeling high levels of anxiety, which stress response do you think you typically have (i.e., Fight, Flight, Freeze, or Fawn)?
- Can you think of a book/show/movie in which someone was having an acute stress response? How did they respond when their amygdala responded to a threat?
- What are beneficial ways that you handle high levels of anxiety?

STORY TIME

Hand out coloring sheets and crayons or markers to younger students while the facilitator reads the story, if desired.

Panic in the Park

Annie loved being independent. To her, being able to do things on her own was proof that she was growing up and responsible. She loved running errands for her family, she loved riding her bike on her own, and she especially loved walking to visit her friends who lived in her neighborhood. She also knew that part of being grown up and responsible was being able to understand how to keep herself safe.

One afternoon, Annie was walking home from visiting her friend George, who lived two streets away from her. She had taken all the right safety precautions. She texted her parents that she was on her way, then she took the same route she always did, waiting for the pedestrian crossing lights at every intersection. The last part of her walk home was through a park that was right behind her family's apartment. The park was Annie's favorite part of her walk, as it was usually peaceful and calm.

As Annie entered the park, she saw an unfamiliar dog running in her direction. A jumble of thoughts entered Annie's head all at once. The dog was larger than her, it was not on a leash, and there did not seem to be an owner nearby. Annie began to panic, and several ideas rushed into her head at once.

- *I might be able to defend myself if the dog attacks me.*
- *I think I could outrun the dog, get to one of the big trees, and climb up out of the dog's reach.*
- *I could stop right here and see if the dog chooses to go another direction if I don't look interesting.*
- *I could give the dog the rest of my snack to keep it from attacking me.*

While none of these options seemed best, Annie's brain was urging her to protect herself as quickly as possible. In a split second, Annie started to run toward the nearest tree. The dog continued running toward her. Annie clumsily jumped into the tree and climbed up a few branches. As soon as she was safely out of the dog's reach, the owners came running up behind the dog. They apologized that their dog had scared Annie. The dog had escaped out of their backyard, and they had been in a game of chase for an hour.

Once the dog was leashed, Annie breathed a sigh of relief, climbed down, and made her way home at last.

DISCUSSION QUESTIONS

- Annie's four ideas to keep herself safe are examples of Fight, Flight, Freeze, and Fawn responses. Can you identify each one? How do you know?
- What do you think of the response Annie chose? Which do you think you would have done?
- Was Annie in real or perceived danger? Use information from the story to support your opinion.

SKILL PRACTICE

Ask students how they might apply what they learned from Annie's experience walking home, giving every student a chance to answer one question. Skill practice can be adapted to allow students to answer in pairs or to record on the worksheet.

How might your brain respond if:

- Someone is sitting in your assigned seat?
- A person you do not know is rude to you?
- A friend tells you they are angry with you over text/social media?
- Your teacher gives you negative feedback on your homework assignment?
- Someone is riding directly toward you on their bike on a narrow sidewalk?
- A coach yells at the team during a game?
- You make a mistake, and you have to tell someone about it?

ADDITIONAL ACTIVITIES

- Using the skills practice questions, have students pick one or two of the examples and brainstorm what a Fight, Flight, Freeze, and Fawn response would look like in their selected scenario(s). Students can work in pairs or threes. Have students share with the group if time permits.
- Have students split a paper into two columns labeled "real danger" and "imaginary danger." Ask students to think through the difference between the two and come up with 3–5 examples for each column. Open the group up for discussion and talk through their examples, giving feedback as needed.

CLOSING CONSIDERATIONS

Our brain is wired to protect us and keep us safe. This means that we will all experience the Fight, Flight, Freeze, or Fawn response from time to time. However, it is important to recognize the difference between real and imagined danger. This way, if our amygdala is activated in response to imagined danger, we can learn to use coping skills to respond more appropriately and see situations more accurately.

Ask students to summarize the content of the lesson in one sentence. In pairs or groups of three, students may share their answers. If time allows, a few students may share with the whole group. Ask students to notice if/when their Fight, Flight, Freeze, or Fawn response is activated this week or if they observe it in someone else.

FIGHT, FLIGHT, FREEZE, OR FAWN RESPONSE

Source: 15-Minute Focus: Anxiety Workbook by Dr. Leigh Bagwell

"WOULD YOU RATHER?" GAME

Playing the "Would You Rather?" game is a fun and engaging activity for students to develop their critical thinking skills. Students will reflect on their experience, evaluate their options based on their preferences, and reflect on the opinions of others, providing a different perspective and strengthening their sense of connection to one another.

Would You Rather?

Copy and cut out the questions for small groups to discuss, or have students stand in the center of the room and move towards one side or the other to show their vote for either option as the facilitator reads the questions aloud.

- WOULD YOU RATHER FIGHT SOMEONE WHO IS BEING MEAN TO YOU OR IGNORE THE PERSON?

- WOULD YOU RATHER BE ALONE WHEN YOU ARE STRESSED OR ENGAGE WITH OTHERS?

- WOULD YOU RATHER LEAVE THE ROOM WHEN SOMEONE IS UPSET OR STAY WITH THEM WHILE THEY HAVE BIG FEELINGS?

- WOULD YOU RATHER FIGHT WITH A FRIEND YOU DISAGREE WITH OR IGNORE IT UNTIL YOU BOTH FORGET ABOUT IT?

- WOULD YOU RATHER APPROACH SOMEONE WHO IS ANGRY AND HELP THEM FEEL BETTER OR LET THEM FIGURE IT OUT THEMSELVES?

- WOULD YOU RATHER PHYSICALLY LEAVE A PLACE WHERE A FIGHT IS HAPPENING OR STAY AND WATCH IT UNFOLD?

> *Go easy on yourself.*
> *Whatever you do today, let it be enough.*
> **UNKNOWN**

Your Body on Anxiety

MIND MAP

On the board, draw a mind map and ask students to consider the meaning of *Brain*.

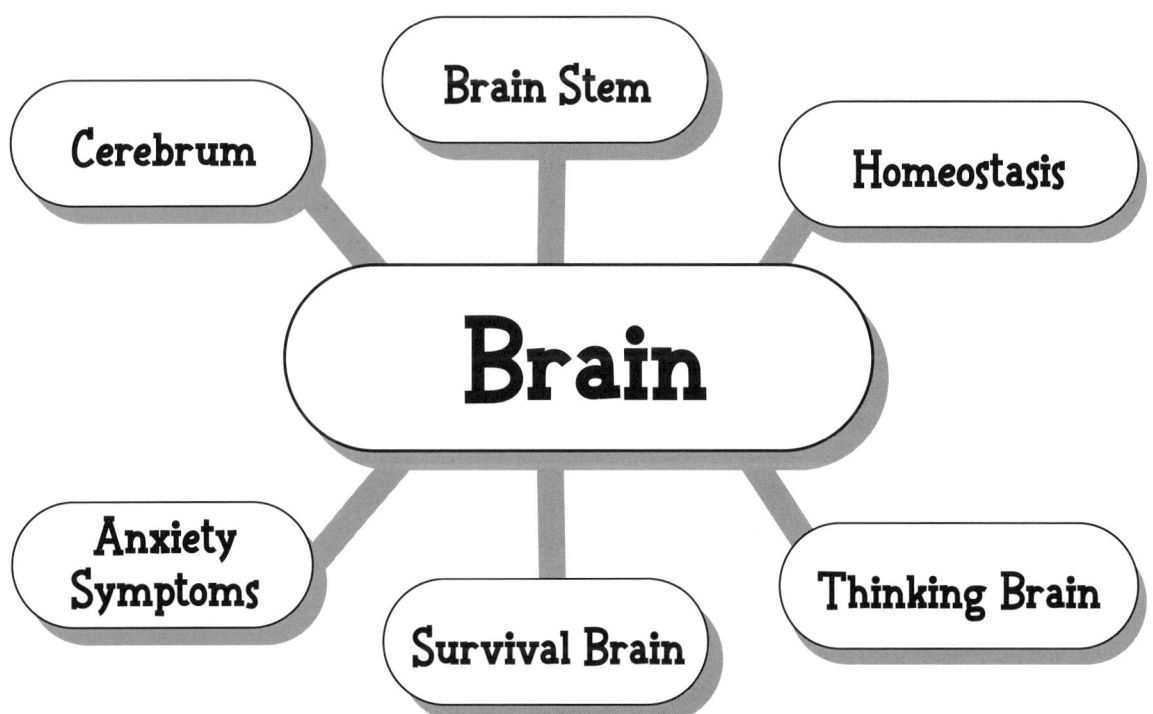

ASCA® STANDARDS

- **B-SMS 1.** Responsibility for self and actions
- **B-SS 4.** Empathy
- **B-SS 8.** Advocacy skills for self and others and ability to assert self, when necessary

DIRECTIONS

- Complete a brief check-in with your students by asking them to share a high and low for the week or by using the weather to represent their emotions.
- Review the Group Expectations.
- Read the Lesson Introduction and ask the Circle Time Questions before reading the Story and asking the Discussion Questions. Students can work in pairs to craft their responses or share with the whole group.
- Complete the Skill Practice, "Would You Rather?" game, and Additional Activities as time allows.
- Be sure to complete the Closing Considerations with each session.

Definitions:

- The **cerebrum**, the Thinking Brain, is the part of the brain that allows us to think about and understand information.
- The **brain stem**, the Survival Brain, controls the sympathetic nervous system that controls functions that keep us alive (breathing, blood flow, muscle movement, etc.)
- **Homeostasis** is when our body is stable and safe physically and emotionally.

LESSON INTRODUCTION

Last time we learned that when we have high levels of anxiety, the amygdala (our Feeling Brain) reacts to the threat to try to protect us. It releases hormones that include adrenaline and noradrenaline.

When these hormones are released, they communicate to the brain stem, our Survival Brain, which controls the sympathetic nervous systems responsible for keeping you alive. The hormones tell your body's systems that they need to stop and focus on the immediate situation. This hormonal release increases your heart rate, blood pressure, and breathing. In turn, these changes in the body's homeostasis let those systems know they will have to work effectively and efficiently to find or create a safe environment. When this happens, the amygdala also sends messages to the cerebrum, our Thinking Brain, to shut down so that all of the body's energy and attention can focus on surviving the threat. When this happens, it is almost impossible to think rationally about the situation.

What does anxiety look like when it happens? We can have different kinds of symptoms depending on our response to the threat. We may feel symptoms in our bodies, in the way we feel, and in the way we act.

Physical symptoms often include increased heart rate, tense muscles, increased blood pressure, excessive sweating, rapid breathing, headaches, nausea, digestive issues, poor sleep, feeling jittery or lightheaded, a hot face, clammy hands, or a dry mouth.

Emotional symptoms often include feeling afraid, worried, or nervous; constant worries or concerns about family, school, friends, or activities; repetitive, unwanted thoughts or actions; fears or embarrassment or making mistakes, low self-esteem, lack of self-confidence, or crying.

Behavioral symptoms often include refusing to talk; clinging to parents, guardians, siblings, or trusted adults; acting scared or upset, startling easily, missing school, refusing to do things, avoiding people, and having tantrums.

It is also important to note that once a threatening situation has been resolved, our bodies must reset themselves to return to homeostasis. Science has shown that after a threat (real or imaginary) is gone, it takes between twenty to sixty minutes for the body to calm down. However, when we know what anxiety feels like, we can intervene and use positive coping skills to keep it from escalating and getting worse.

CIRCLE TIME QUESTIONS

Ask students to reflect and share their answers to the following questions with the group.

- What physical, emotional, and/or behavioral symptoms of anxiety have you experienced?
- Have you ever needed extra time to calm down after being anxious?
- What is the most common symptom of anxiety you feel?

STORY TIME

Hand out coloring sheets and crayons or markers to younger students while the facilitator reads the story, if desired.

Busted Bus Ride

> Max loved school but did not like to ride the bus. Unfortunately, his parents were not able to take him to school and he did not live close enough to walk. Every time he boarded the bus, it felt like he was entering a dark, crowded tunnel—and the smells, the sights, and the sounds did not make it any better. Everyone was so loud, the windows barely opened, and he could smell all the odors from the bus.
>
> Everyday Max's goal on his bus ride was to just make it through, but sometimes it was harder than others. Today, when Max boarded the bus to school, he put his earbuds in right away. His bus driver, Ms. Dryer, said hi, but Max did not respond. He just wanted to focus on his music. As he made his way to his seat, the bus seemed to be even darker and more crowded than usual. He felt a wave of heat rush from his face all the way down his body. He started to sweat and as hard as he tried to take deep breaths, he could not. It felt like it took forever to find an empty spot. When he sat down, he stared out the window, ignoring everyone.
>
> Once they arrived at school and Max escaped the bus, he felt like he could breathe again. After recentering himself during homeroom, he was ready for his day. However, when the bus announcements began at the end of the school day, he started to fill with dread once again.
>
> When his bus was called and he dragged himself outside, Max was surprised to see Ms. Dyer was outside the bus, smiling at him and waving. He took out his earbuds and walked over to her before going up the bus steps.

> "Max, I've noticed you don't really seem comfortable on the bus, and I wanted to help figure out some ways to make it easier for you," Ms. Dyer said.
>
> Max was so surprised she knew but was ultimately grateful. As the rest of the kids boarded the bus, Ms. Dyer and Max came up with a plan together. She would save him a seat in one of the front rows. When it was good weather, the window would already be open to give him some fresh air. And they would check-in every couple of weeks to see how it was going.
>
> It was not perfect, but Max knew he was going to be okay. And if he was not, he knew it was okay to ask Ms. Dyer for help.

DISCUSSION QUESTIONS

- What were Max's symptoms of anxiety? Think about the physical, emotional, and behavioral symptoms you observed in the story.
- What do you think of Max and Ms. Dyer's plan to help his anxiety?
- What role did Ms. Dyer play in helping Max understand himself? How might this help Max advocate for himself in the future?

SKILL PRACTICE

Ask students how they might apply what Max learned about his anxiety, giving every student a chance to answer one question. Skill practice can be adapted to allow students to answer in pairs or record their answers on the worksheet.

How might your body respond:

- If you had to recite a poem in front of the class?
- When you are at home in your room doing something you love?
- When you have to ask a clerk a question at the store?
- If a server brought out the wrong meal for you at a restaurant?
- When you have to walk in the crowded hallway between classes?
- When you are hanging out with your best friend?
- If you have to introduce yourself to someone new?
- If you need to raise your hand in class to ask a question?

ADDITIONAL ACTIVITIES

- Distribute the **How Anxiety Feels in My Body Worksheet** and colored pencils, markers, or crayons to students. They can color it as time allows. The student will identify where they feel anxiety in their body. Students should write anxiety symptoms they experience in the bubbles, then draw lines from each bubble to where they feel each symptom in their body. For emotional symptoms such as sadness, they could draw a line to their heart. For behavioral symptoms such as running away, they can draw a line to their feet. It is okay for students to draw more than one line to the same area of the body. Once all students have had time to identify their personal anxiety symptoms, discuss what symptoms they have in common and which ones are different.

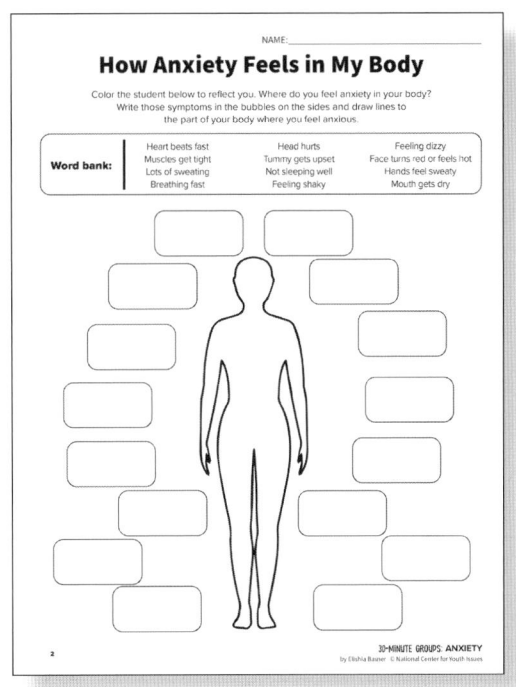

- Have students draw three columns on a page and have them title the columns "Physical," "Emotional," and "Behavior." Ask students to write down any symptoms of anxiety they notice during the next week. The goal is to increase their awareness of how their bodies are warning them of increasing anxiety.

CLOSING CONSIDERATIONS

One of the most helpful things we can do to manage our anxiety is to understand how it feels in our body. Taking the time to understand how both our brain and body respond when we are anxious is the first step to increasing our ability to reduce our anxiety and choose appropriate coping skills when we do feel anxious.

Ask students to summarize the content of this lesson in one sentence. In pairs or groups of three, students may share their answers. If time allows, a few students may share with the whole group. Ask students to notice how anxiety shows up in their bodies and what it feels like this week, or if they observe it in someone else.

"WOULD YOU RATHER?" GAME

Playing the "Would You Rather?" game is a fun and engaging activity for students to develop their critical thinking skills. Students will reflect on their experience, evaluate their options based on their preferences, and reflect on the opinions of others, providing a different perspective and strengthening their sense of connection to one another.

Would You Rather?

Copy and cut out the questions for small groups to discuss, or have students stand in the center of the room and move towards one side or the other to show their vote for either option as the facilitator reads the questions aloud.

WOULD YOU RATHER ASK A QUESTION IN FRONT OF THE CLASS OR HAVE A PRIVATE CONVERSATION WITH THE TEACHER?

WOULD YOU RATHER FEEL BAD IN SILENCE OR TELL SOMEONE HOW YOU FEEL?

WOULD YOU RATHER IGNORE THE PHYSICAL SIGNS OF ANXIETY OR UNDERSTAND WHAT YOUR BODY IS TRYING TO TELL YOU?

WOULD YOU RATHER UNDERSTAND YOUR RESPONSE TO THINGS THAT MAKE YOU NERVOUS OR NOT KNOW WHY YOUR BODY IS RESPONDING LIKE IT DOES?

WOULD YOU RATHER HAVE SOMEONE OFFER YOU HELP OR ASK FOR HELP YOURSELF?

WOULD YOU RATHER BELIEVE YOUR ANXIOUS THOUGHTS OR FIND A WAY TO MANAGE THEM?

Types of Anxiety

MIND MAP

On the board, draw a mind map and ask students to consider the meaning of *Anxiety*.

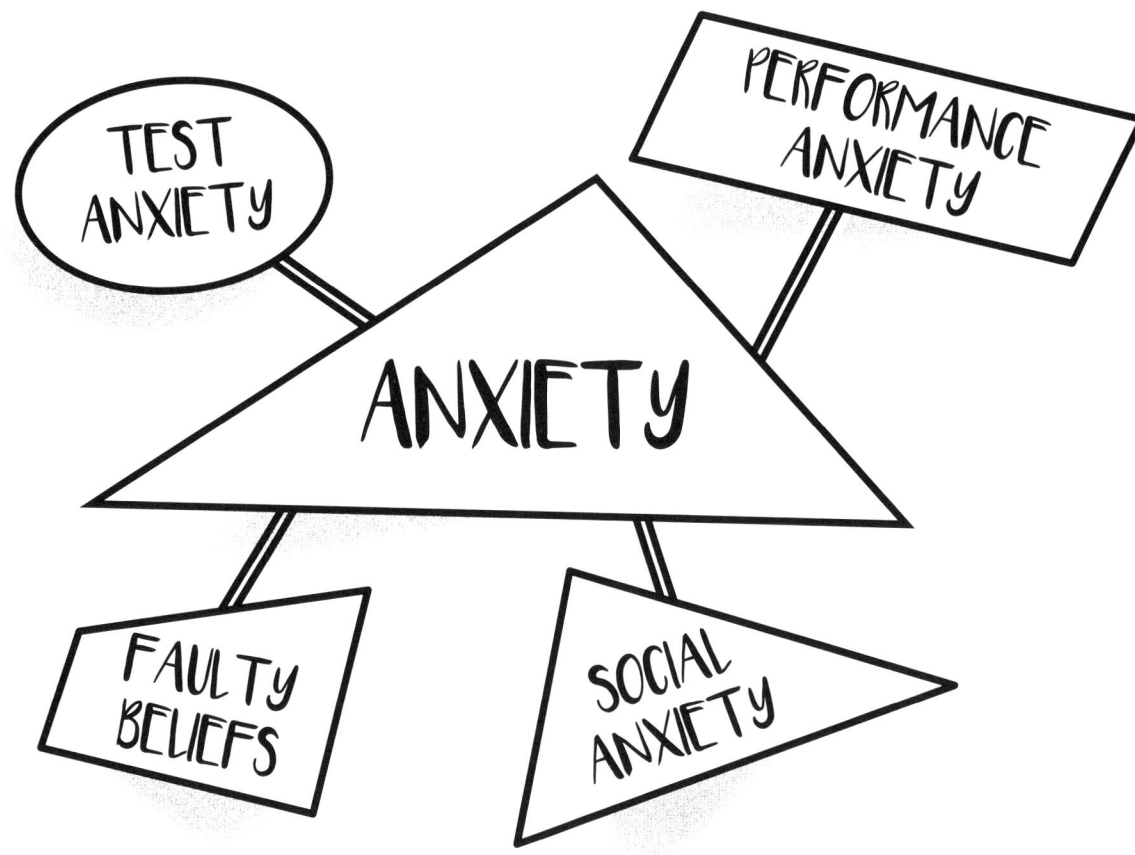

ASCA® STANDARDS

- **B-SS 2.** Positive, respectful, and supportive relationships with students who are similar to and different from them
- **B-SS 3.** Positive relationships with adults to support success
- **B-SMS 6.** Ability to identify and overcome barriers

DIRECTIONS

- Complete a brief check-in with your students by asking them to share a high and low for the week or by using the weather to represent their emotions.
- Review the Group Expectations.
- Read the Lesson Introduction and ask the Circle Time Questions before reading the Story and asking the Discussion Questions. Students can work in pairs to craft their responses or share with the whole group.
- Complete the Skill Practice, "Would You Rather?" game, and Additional Activities as time allows.
- Be sure to complete the Closing Considerations with each session.

Definitions:

- **Test Anxiety** is a specific type of anxiety that occurs in response to the anticipation of, during, or after, academic assessments, tests, or exams.
- **Social Anxiety** is an anxiety disorder characterized by an intense fear of social situations and interactions.
- **Performance Anxiety** is a type of anxiety that typically develops in anticipation of or during presentations, performances, or competitive situations.
- **Faulty Beliefs** are thoughts that we have based on inaccurate or irrational information.

LESSON INTRODUCTION

We have been talking a lot about general anxiety. However, anxiety can also be related to very specific situations. Today we are going to talk about three specific types of anxiety: test anxiety, social anxiety, and performance anxiety. Many of the symptoms people experience with these specific types of anxiety are common to general anxiety. However, the difference is that they tend to be driven by specific situations.

For example, **test anxiety** is tied to the fear of performing poorly on exams and assessments. If you experience test anxiety, you might experience symptoms such as ruminating (thinking over and over) over poor performance, excessively worrying about failing, and hyper-focusing on getting the results of the test. There may be different reasons we are afraid of failing a test. Some fears about failing are valid, and some fears are based on faulty thinking. Therefore, knowing why we are afraid of failing a test will help us to control and reduce test anxiety.

Social anxiety is characterized by an intense fear of social situations, as well as an often irrational fear of negative evaluation or rejection by others. Those who suffer from social anxiety worry about being judged, embarrassed, or humiliated in front of others, leading them to avoid many social situations. Specific symptoms include avoidance of social situations, refusal to participate in class discussions or presentations, avoidance of situations where one is the center of attention, blushing, trembling, or sweating, avoiding eye contact, panic attacks, increased heartbeat, nausea, and profound distress. Again, when we understand where the fear of being judged or humiliated comes from, we are able to better manage social anxiety.

Finally, **performance anxiety** is a type of anxiety that typically develops in anticipation of or during presentations, performances, or competitive situations. It can particularly affect students in areas such as public speaking, visual and theater arts, sports, and competitions. It often involves worries about being evaluated or making mistakes during the performance. The symptoms of performance anxiety are similar to test and social anxiety. In some cases, a person may avoid the performance or competition or may dedicate an excessive amount of time and energy to practicing. They often sacrifice many other activities and responsibilities, like playing with friends, eating, and even taking care of themselves, to use that time to prepare for the performance.

Understanding our general anxiety is important. However, it is also important to understand whether your anxiety is focused on a particular area. This deeper self-awareness will help you create more specific and effective coping skills, as well as target faulty thinking (which we are going to focus on in the next two sessions).

CIRCLE TIME QUESTIONS

Ask students to reflect and share their answers to the following questions with the group. Larger groups may need to be broken into smaller groups to give students ample time to share their answers and deepen the conversation.

- Do you have experience with one of these more specific types of anxiety?
- Have you noticed any patterns in the things that cause you anxiety?
- What kinds of fears related to tests, social situations, and/or performance have you experienced?

STORY TIME

Hand out coloring sheets and crayons or markers to younger students while the facilitator reads the story, if desired.

Science Spiral

> Jacinta prides herself on being an excellent student who gets good grades. She has A's in almost all of her classes, and it is very important to her that she is able to stay on the honor roll. In fact, she thinks about this all the time, and even though she has been able to keep her high grades, she is often worried that just one misstep will ruin everything.
>
> She is taking a science class, and it has been more challenging for her than she has experienced in the past, and she feels more stress than usual about her grades. She has an A so far, but she has decided to take every opportunity for extra credit. She retakes tests, attends tutoring, and studies with others as often as she can. She has stopped sitting with her friends at lunch to drill herself with flashcards. One Friday, her friend Jamie invited her over, which Jacinta typically would have been excited to do, but she refused, saying she needed to study over the weekend.
>
> Jamie was surprised by her friend's response.

"I feel like all you do is study anymore. Don't you have an A?" she asked.

"Yes, but I can't risk not doing well on even one assignment!" Jacinta replied.

"Why not?" asked Jamie. When Jacinta did not have an answer for her, Jamie walked away.

Jacinta was taken aback. As she reflected on Jamie's parting question, Jacinta realized that perhaps there was something bigger going on than just wanting to do well. She realized that every time she walked into science class, her hands started to sweat, and her thoughts started to go in circles about whether or not she would do well in class.

She put down her flashcards and decided she needed to talk to an adult. Jacinta went straight to the school counselor's office. Something needed to change.

DISCUSSION QUESTIONS

- What type(s) of specific anxiety was Jacinta dealing with? Use evidence from the story to support your answer.
- What coping skills was Jacinta using to try and manage her anxiety? Were they effective or ineffective?
- What do you think of her decision at the end of the story to go to the school counselor?

SKILL PRACTICE

Ask students how they might apply what Jacinta learned about her experience with anxiety, giving every student a chance to answer one question. Skill practice can be adapted to allow students to answer in pairs or record on the worksheet.

What specific kind of anxiety is showing up if:

- You are constantly worried about getting bad grades?
- You feel if you make a mistake, it is the end of the world?
- You are nervous that everyone around you is judging you?
- The pressure of a good grade seems to overtake your mind, making it difficult to remember what you have learned?
- You get a stomachache when someone invites you to a party?
- You are often comparing yourself to others on social media?
- You keep trying to avoid competitive games in PE class?
- You find yourself believing that if something is not perfect, then you are a failure?

ADDITIONAL ACTIVITIES

- Have students draw four columns on a piece of paper with the following labels: Academic, Emotional, Physical, Social. Explain how specific anxieties can impact us in these ways just like general anxiety. Have students pick a specific anxiety most relevant to them and ask them to suggest ways this anxiety affects them in each of the categories. This is a good time to reinforce their courageous choice in asking for support.

- Distribute the **Performance Anxiety Management Pledge Worksheet** and assist the students in identifying how they can appropriately recover if they make a mistake during their next performance. When finished, allow students to share their Performance Anxiety Management Pledges with each other. Remind the group that they can help each other honor their pledges with encouragement and support.

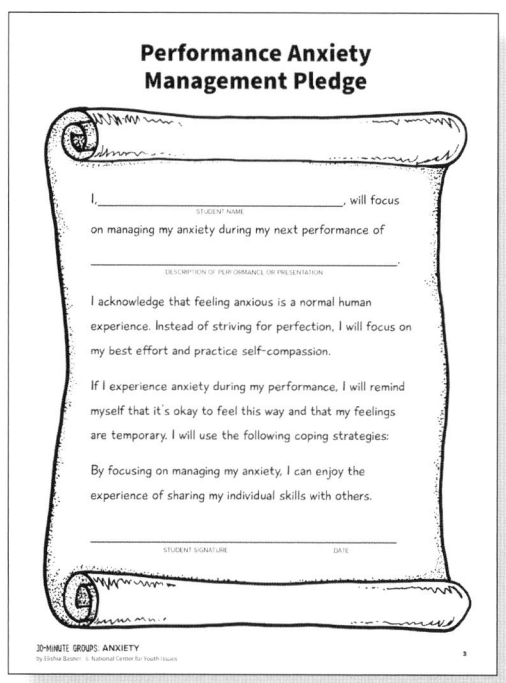

CLOSING CONSIDERATIONS

Anxiety can show up for different reasons and in different ways in everyone. It is important to notice if your anxiety seems to be related to specific patterns, triggers, or situations. These can be related to things like tests, social activities, and performances. Regardless, it is important to understand that very often, these types of anxiety are based on faulty beliefs and that asking an adult for help can help us work through these beliefs and cope.

Ask students to summarize the content of the lesson in one sentence. In pairs or groups of three, students may share their answers. If time allows, a few students may share with the whole group. Ask students to notice if/when their anxiety response is activated by more specific situations this week related to test anxiety, social anxiety, or performance anxiety.

"WOULD YOU RATHER?" GAME

Playing the "Would You Rather?" game is a fun and engaging activity for students to develop their critical thinking skills. Students will reflect on their experience, evaluate their options based on their preferences, and reflect on the opinions of others, providing a different perspective and strengthening their sense of connection to one another.

Would You Rather?

Copy and cut out the questions for small groups to discuss, or have students stand in the center of the room and move towards one side or the other to show their vote for either option as the facilitator reads the questions aloud.

- WOULD YOU RATHER TAKE A TEST OR WRITE A PAPER TO DEMONSTRATE YOUR KNOWLEDGE?

- WOULD YOU RATHER HAVE A LOT OF GOOD FRIENDSHIPS OR ONLY HAVE ONE OR TWO GOOD FRIENDS?

- WOULD YOU RATHER TRY TO FIT IN WITH OTHERS ON SOCIAL MEDIA OR BE CONFIDENT IN YOUR OWN UNIQUE QUALITIES?

- WOULD YOU RATHER WIN EVERY COMPETITION OR AVOID BEING COMPETITIVE AT ALL?

- WOULD YOU RATHER ASK A TEACHER/COUNSELOR FOR HELP OR DO EVERYTHING ON YOUR OWN?

- WOULD YOU RATHER BE COMFORTABLE AT A PARTY OR STAY AT HOME SO YOU DO NOT HAVE TO GO TO PARTIES?

30-MINUTE GROUPS: ANXIETY MANAGEMENT

> *Once you realize there is life after mistakes, you gain self-confidence that never goes away.*
> **BOB SCHIEFFER**

CHAPTER 5

The Think-Feel-Do Cycle

MIND MAP

On the board, draw a mind map and ask students to consider the meaning of *Think-Feel-Do*.

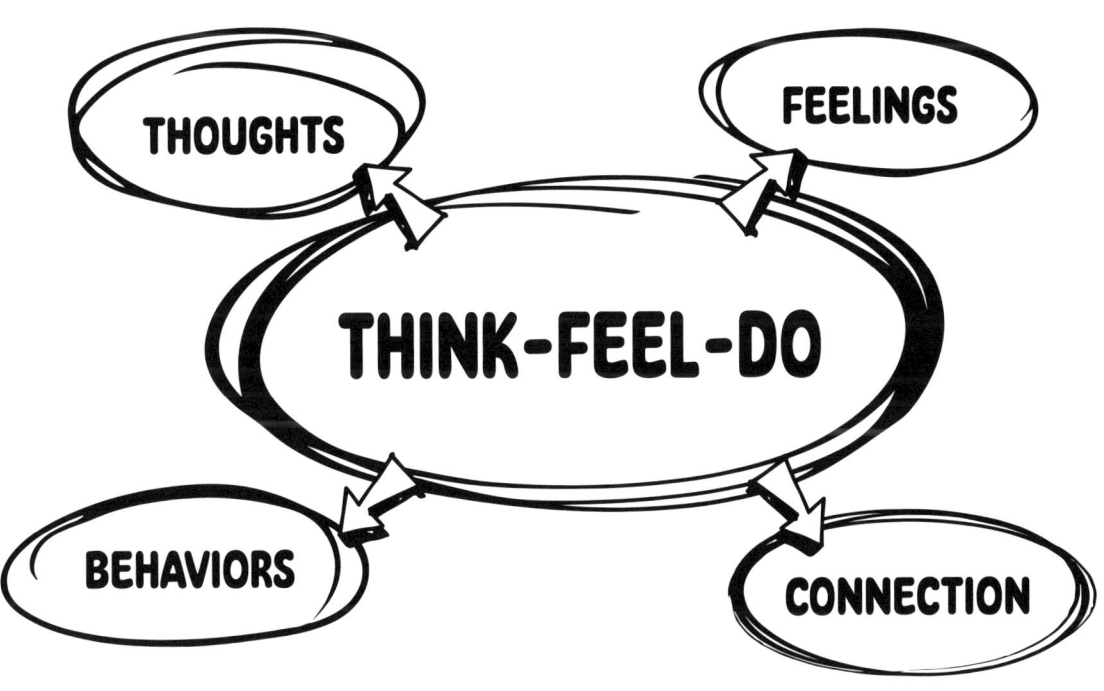

ASCA® STANDARDS

- **B-LS 1.** Critical thinking skills to make informed decisions
- **B-SS 2.** Positive, respectful, and supportive relationships with students who are similar to and different from them
- **B-SMS 6.** Ability to identify and overcome barriers

DIRECTIONS

- Complete a brief check-in with your students by asking them to share a high and low for the week or by using the weather to represent their emotions.
- Review the Group Expectations.
- Read the Lesson Introduction and ask the Circle Time Questions before reading the Story and asking the Discussion Questions. Students can work in pairs to craft their responses or share with the whole group.
- Complete the Skill Practice, "Would You Rather?" game, and Additional Activities as time allows.
- Be sure to complete the Closing Considerations with each session.

Definitions:

- A **triggering event** is a real or perceived threat that is likely to increase your anxiety.
- The **Think-Feel-Do Cycle** is an approach that helps us understand how our thoughts, feelings, and behaviors influence one another.

LESSON INTRODUCTION

There is a relationship between our thoughts, feelings, and behaviors. We call this the **Think-Feel-Do Cycle**. When you experience a triggering event, the way you feel about the event will often depend on what you think about that event. Your feelings cause you to behave in a certain way. A triggering event is something that is likely to increase your anxiety. If you notice any of the signs and symptoms of anxiety, it is likely that you are experiencing a triggering event.

Even if you are not sure what to do, noticing and making the connection between your thoughts, feelings, and actions and your anxiety is the first step toward progress and change—especially when it comes to your thoughts.

CIRCLE TIME QUESTIONS

Ask students to reflect and share their answers to the following questions.

Think about a recent triggering event for your anxiety and answer the following questions:

- What was happening in your environment?
- What thoughts did you have?
- What feelings did you have?
- What action did you take?

STORY TIME

Hand out coloring sheets and crayons or markers to younger students while the facilitator reads the story, if desired.

Running Thoughts

Xavier hated running, and dreaded the mile run in PE class every year. It almost always happened in the winter, so he could ignore it for a while. However, when the temperatures began to drop, he started to get nervous. The mile run would be here soon.

During the weeks leading up to the run, Xavier's teacher, Mr. Plotnick, would encourage the students to practice jogging at the beginning of class and show them other exercises that would help prepare them for the event. Xavier thought this just prolonged the torture; he wanted it just to be over as soon as possible and that was all he could think about.

On the day of the mile run, Xavier, who was normally friendly with all his classmates, did not want to talk to anyone. His thinking was only focused on the run. Thoughts like, "*Ugh. This is such a stupid requirement*" and "*This is going to be the worst gym class ever*" ran through his head. His hands were clammy, and his heart was beating fast before he even started running.

Just before Mr. Plotnick started the run, he gave a pep talk.

"All right, class. I know that some of you are excited to run, but many wish you did not have to do this. I was like you when I was your age. I hated running. I hated being sweaty. I hated being out of breath. And that was all I could think about. Then one day, a teacher approached me and asked me a question that would change my outlook. The question was: "What if you changed the way you talked about running in your head?" And in that moment, I realized if I told myself that it was going to be horrible, I was going to be right. But if I told myself I was going to make it and it was not going to be that bad… well, what if that could be true too?"

As Mr. Plotnick began the countdown to start, Xavier paused to listen to his thoughts. While he was not sure he would ever enjoy running, he was willing to try something that might make it feel slightly less awful.

"Three, two, one…go!" shouted Mr. Plotnick.

"*Maybe this won't be the worst class ever,*" thought Xavier.

And then he started to run.

DISCUSSION QUESTIONS

- How was Xavier's thinking influencing his feelings and behavior?
- How do you think Xavier's mile run felt after he changed his thoughts? Do you think he felt better or worse afterward than he had in the past?
- What types of situations could Xavier apply this strategy to in the future?

SKILL PRACTICE

Ask students how they might apply what Xavier learned about changing his thoughts to better control his feelings and actions, giving every student a chance to answer one question. Skill practice can be adapted to allow students to answer in pairs or record their answers on the worksheet.

How might your thinking be influencing your feelings and behavior:

- If you are dreading an upcoming event?
- When you are excited about an upcoming vacation?
- When the teacher asks you to help with a task you like or dislike in class?
- If you are having a hard time getting along with a sibling or a friend?
- When you are upset about something your caregivers have asked you to do?
- If you are avoiding someone who you had a recent argument with?
- If you are happy about your classes for the quarter/year?
- If you find thunderstorms frightening?

ADDITIONAL ACTIVITIES

- As a group, have the students respond to some prompts with a thumb-up (positive), thumb-down (negative), or thumb-sideways (neutral) based on how they think about certain events they might run into during their everyday lives. For example, running a mile, doing a math problem, reading in front of others, taking tests, going to the store, or socializing in the hall between classes. Point out that though they may have agreed with one another on some things, their thinking is individual to them. This means that the events themselves are not good or bad, but the way we think about them makes them feel one way or the other.

- Have the students write down something they love and something they greatly dislike. Then have them write down the thoughts they associate with each one. If time allows, they can share in pairs or with the larger group. Point out the differences and help them reflect on how these thoughts influence their feelings and behaviors.

CLOSING CONSIDERATIONS

It is important to remember that how we think about things influences how we feel and what we do. If we can understand our thoughts, then we can change them. (More on this next session!)

Ask students to summarize the content of the lesson in one sentence. In pairs or groups of three, students may share their answers. If time allows, a few students may share with the whole group. Ask students to notice their thinking in the coming week, particularly when they feel anxious. What thoughts are they having when a triggering event occurs? Do they notice any patterns?

"WOULD YOU RATHER?" GAME

Playing the "Would You Rather?" game is a fun and engaging activity for students to develop their critical thinking skills. Students will reflect on their experience, evaluate their options based on their preferences, and reflect on the opinions of others, providing a different perspective and strengthening their sense of connection to one another.

Would You Rather?

Copy and cut out the questions for small groups to discuss, or have students stand in the center of the room and move towards one side or the other to show their vote for either option as the facilitator reads the questions aloud.

- WOULD YOU RATHER CONTROL YOUR THOUGHTS OR HAVE YOUR THOUGHTS CONTROL YOU?

- WOULD YOU RATHER FEEL YOUR FEELINGS OR AVOID THEM?

- WOULD YOU RATHER UNDERSTAND THE REASON BEHIND YOUR CHOICES OR CHOOSE WITHOUT UNDERSTANDING?

- WOULD YOU RATHER THINK NEGATIVELY OR POSITIVELY ABOUT MOST THINGS?

- WOULD YOU RATHER BE FILLED WITH DREAD ABOUT THINGS YOU DO NOT LIKE OR FIND A WAY TO REFRAME THEM SO THEY ARE NOT SO AWFUL?

- WOULD YOU RATHER BE ABLE TO MAKE DIFFERENT CHOICES WHEN YOU ARE UPSET OR KEEP MAKING THE CHOICE YOU KNOW?

Interrupting the Think-Feel-Do Cycle

MIND MAP

On the board, draw a mind map and ask students to consider the meaning of *Think-Feel-Do*.

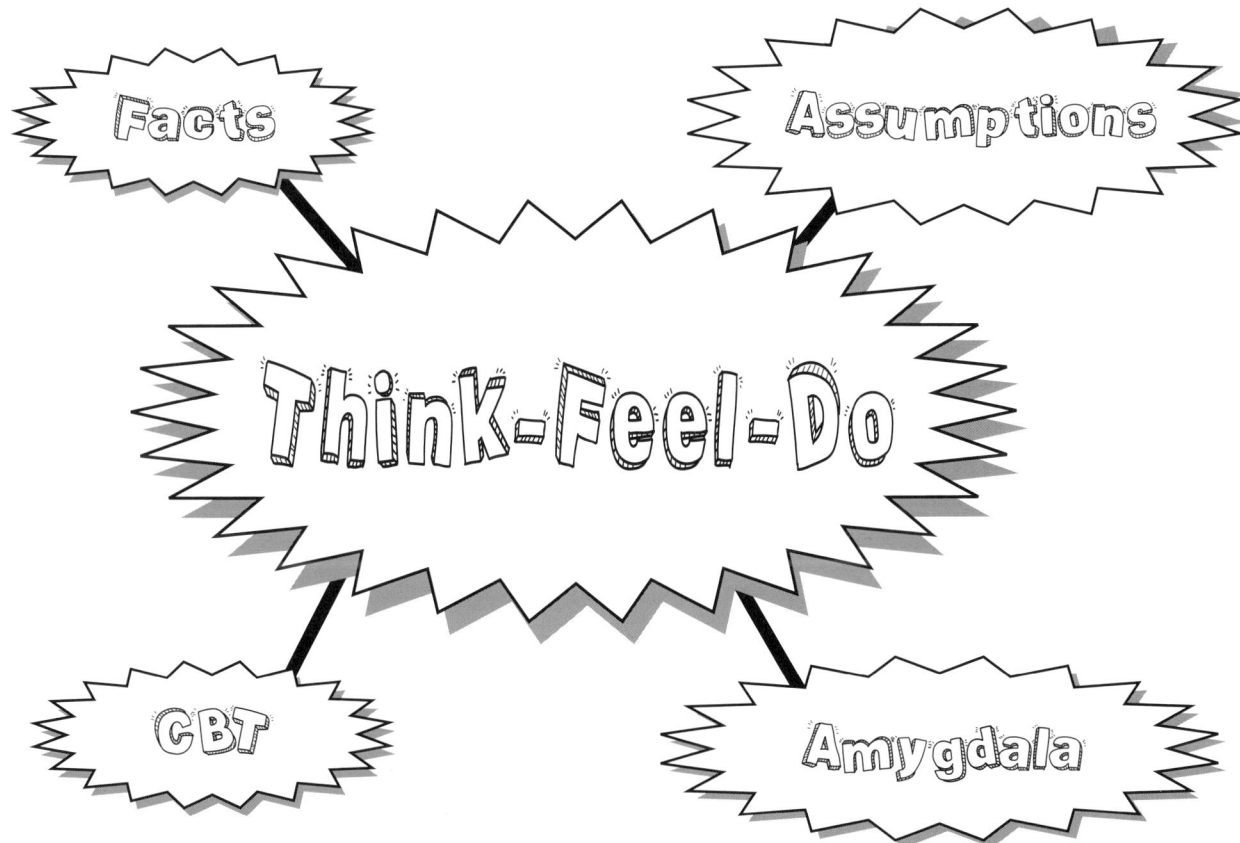

ASCA® STANDARDS

- **B-LS 1.** Critical thinking skills to make informed decisions
- **B-LS 2.** Creative approach to learning, tasks, and problem-solving
- **B-SMS 2.** Self-discipline and self-control
- **B-SMS 7.** Effective coping skills

DIRECTIONS

- Complete a brief check-in with your students by asking them to share a high and low for the week or by using the weather to represent their emotions.

- Review the Group Expectations.

- Read the Lesson Introduction and ask the Circle Time Questions before reading the Story and asking the Discussion Questions. Students can work in pairs to craft their responses or share with the whole group.

- Complete the Skill Practice, "Would You Rather?" game, and Additional Activities as time allows.

- Be sure to complete the Closing Considerations with each session.

Definitions:

- **Facts** are things that are true with proof and evidence to support them.

- **Assumptions** are things believed to be true without any proof or evidence to support them.

LESSON INTRODUCTION

One of the ways that we can manage our anxiety is to interrupt the Think-Feel-Do Cycle we learned about last session.

When we change our anxiety-inducing thoughts, it will help us to reduce our anxious behaviors. Remember the amygdala, our Feeling Brain? When the amygdala senses a threat, it goes into action. So, if we can keep from feeling threatened and afraid, then the amygdala is less likely to be triggered.

Before a triggering event happens, we must slow down and examine our thoughts about potential threats. There are a few questions that can help us determine whether our thoughts are going to send us down a positive or negative path. These questions are:

- Are my thoughts based on facts?

- Do I have all the information necessary to evaluate the situation fairly?

- Would others I trust likely come to the same conclusion?

CIRCLE TIME QUESTIONS

Ask students to reflect and share their answers to the following questions with the group.

- Have you ever had a reaction that was based on faulty thinking and/or big feelings without facts?

- What might have been different had you used the questions we talked about before you reacted?

- What makes it difficult to interrupt the Think-Feel-Do Cycle?

STORY TIME

Hand out coloring sheets and crayons or markers to younger students while the facilitator reads the story, if desired.

Hallway Clarity

One day Destiny saw her two best friends, Mia and Sarah, whispering in the hallway. While that was not so unusual, when she approached them, they quickly stopped talking and giggled. They acted normal from there, but Destiny was uncomfortable.

When they parted ways, Destiny's mind began to spin. *"What had they been talking about that had been so funny? Why did they not let me in on the joke? Were they talking about me? Oh my gosh, they were talking about me! Maybe they don't want to be my friends anymore."* She struggled to focus in class for the rest of the day. Her anxiety burned in her stomach, and she could not seem to recover.

When she got home that afternoon, she confided in her mother that she thought Mia and Sarah no longer wanted to be her friend. She was pretty sure they were talking about her behind her back. Her mother let Destiny finish and then said,

"Destiny, can I ask you a couple questions?"

Destiny nodded.

"Tell me the facts of the situation. Just the facts. Not your thoughts about them."

Destiny recounted what happened in the hallway.

"Okay. Did you ask them what they were talking about? Or do you have any other information about their conversation?"

Destiny shook her head no.

"Now, if Mia or Sarah encountered you whispering with one of them, would you want them to think you did not want to be their friend?"

Destiny's eyes widened in surprise.

"Of course not! They are my best friends in the whole world!"

"Exactly," her mother replied. "Before we jump to the worst conclusion, why don't you go talk to your friends and ask them about what happened?"

Destiny Facetimed them right away, and it turned out they still loved her. They were just talking about a boy Sarah thought was cute, and who was walking right behind Destiny in the hallway.

DISCUSSION QUESTIONS

- How did Destiny's thoughts get out of control?
- Could she have done anything differently to get a more accurate picture sooner?
- What did you think of her mother's questions?

SKILL PRACTICE

Ask students how they might apply what Destiny learned about using facts rather than assumptions to reduce anxiety, giving every student a chance to answer one question. Skill practice can be adapted to allow students to answer in pairs or record their answers on the worksheet.

How could you interrupt the Think-Feel-Do Cycle:

- If you are afraid your friends are talking about you?
- If you feel like your caregivers are mad or disappointed in you?
- When you cannot stop worrying about something bad happening?
- When someone does something out of character or unexpected?
- If your teacher seems annoyed during class?
- If a friend suddenly stops replying to your messages/texts?
- When people hang out without you?
- When others seem like they have much more exciting lives than you on social media?

ADDITIONAL ACTIVITIES

- Choose one of the examples to which the students applied the Think-Feel-Do Cycle earlier. Have them apply these questions at the Think stage of the cycle. Does it lead to different thoughts? Once the students have identified new thoughts, ask them to suggest potential feelings the new thoughts might initiate. Finally, once students have identified new feelings, have them imagine different behaviors they may engage in and compare those to their initial actions. Repeat the process with another example until all students demonstrate an understanding of how changing their thoughts can lead to new feelings and new actions.

- Pass out the age-appropriate **Think-Feel-Do Cycle Poster and Worksheet**. Have them use the handout to examine a triggering event during the coming week and bring their sheet back to the next session. Remember, our bodies can let us know we are experiencing a triggering event through the signs and symptoms of anxiety.

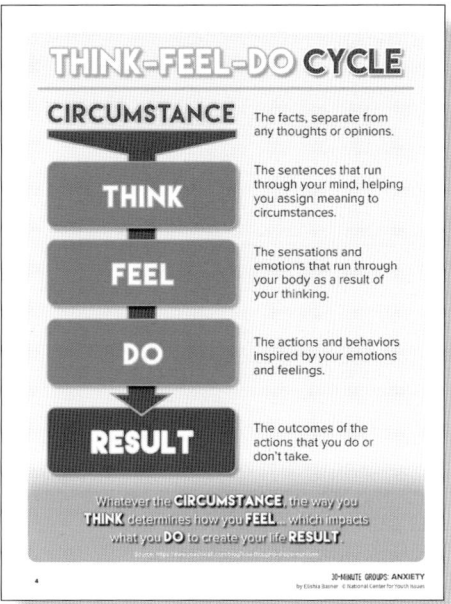

Source: https://www.coachkiah.com/blog/how-thoughts-shape-our-lives

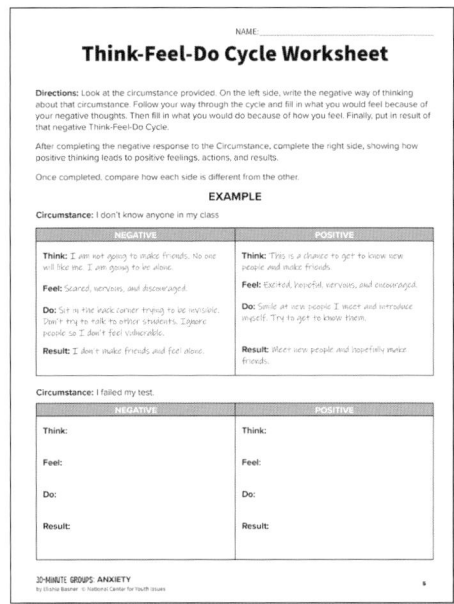
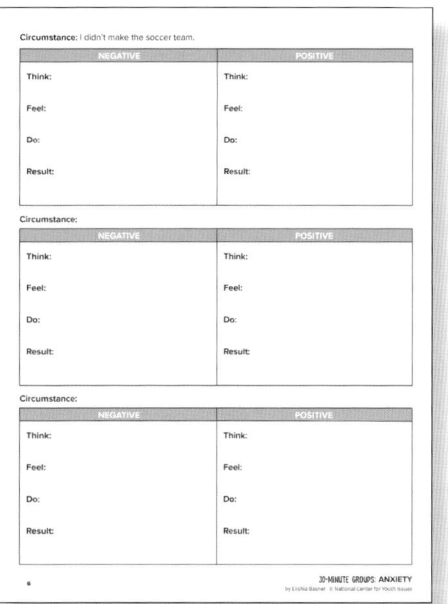

CLOSING CONSIDERATIONS

Remember, the best place to interrupt the Think-Feel-Do Cycle and keep yourself from spiraling with anxiety is before anxiety gets escalated: Think! If you can change your thoughts, you can change your feelings. If you can change your feelings, you can make different, more clearheaded choices. This is how we take control of our emotional well-being! We might not get it right every single time, but even trying is a start.

Ask students to summarize the content of the lesson in one sentence. In pairs or groups of three, students may share their answers. If time allows, a few students may share with the whole group. Ask students to try and interrupt their personal Think-Feel-Do Cycle at least one time in the next week and report back.

"WOULD YOU RATHER?" GAME

Playing the "Would You Rather?" game is a fun and engaging activity for students to develop their critical thinking skills. Students will reflect on their experience, evaluate their options based on their preferences, and reflect on the opinions of others, providing a different perspective and strengthening their sense of connection to one another.

Copy and cut out the questions for small groups to discuss, or have students stand in the center of the room and move towards one side or the other to show their vote for either option as the facilitator reads the questions aloud.

WOULD YOU RATHER INTERRUPT YOUR FAULTY THINKING OR LET IT SPIRAL?

WOULD YOU RATHER ASK FOR CLARIFICATION WHEN SOMETHING GOES WRONG OR REACT TO YOUR FIRST THOUGHT?

WOULD YOU RATHER ASSUME THE BEST- OR WORST-CASE SCENARIO?

WOULD YOU RATHER MAKE A CHOICE FROM YOUR AMYGDALA (FEELING BRAIN) OR YOUR CEREBRUM (THINKING BRAIN)?

WOULD YOU RATHER FEEL IN CONTROL OF YOUR EMOTIONS OR OUT OF CONTROL OF YOUR EMOTIONS?

WOULD YOU RATHER STOP BEING SOMEONE'S FRIEND BASED ON SOMETHING YOU OBSERVED OR GET MORE INFORMATION BEFORE YOU DECIDE WHAT TO DO?

Coping Skills – Mindfulness

MIND MAP

On the board, draw a mind map and ask students to consider the meaning of *Coping Skills*.

- CALM
- MINDFULNESS
- **COPING SKILLS**
- AWARENESS
- BEING PRESENT

ASCA® STANDARDS

- **B-SMS 7.** Effective coping skills
- **B-SMS 10.** Ability to manage transitions and adapt to change
- **B-SS 3.** Positive relationships with adults to support success
- **B-SS 9.** Social maturity and behaviors appropriate to the situation and environment

DIRECTIONS

- Complete a brief check-in with your students by asking them to share a high and low for the week or by using the weather to represent their emotions.
- Review the Group Expectations.
- Read the Lesson Introduction and ask the Circle Time Questions before reading the Story and asking the Discussion Questions. Students can work in pairs to craft their responses or share with the whole group.
- Complete the Skill Practice, "Would You Rather?" game, and Additional Activities as time allows.
- Be sure to complete the Closing Considerations with each session.

Definitions:

- **Mindfulness** is the act of being present and being intentional with our attention.

LESSON INTRODUCTION

If you struggle with anxiety, it is important to understand the strategies that can help you better manage it. These coping skills will help us feel more in control of ourselves when feeling anxious or overwhelmed. It is important to have a variety of coping skills so we can use them in all different kinds of situations and settings. For the next three sessions, we will explore various effective coping skills for managing anxiety.

First, we are going to talk about **mindfulness**. Mindful activities can help us slow down and pay more attention to thoughts, feelings, and behaviors that often lead to anxiety. When we experience anxiety, we often feel intense emotions and energy.

When we are mindful, we are present with our bodies and our environment. Mindfulness helps us to:

- Pay attention to what is happening in and around us.
- Focus on the present moment.
- Do one thing at a time.
- Give our brain a break from worrying.
- Keep our feelings from taking over.
- Refrain from being critical or judgmental of ourselves.

When we practice mindfulness, we use all five senses (sight, hearing, smell, feeling, taste) to focus on our immediate environment and situation. We can use mindful activities to help us when we experience a high level of anxiety. It will help our brain to calm down, and the anxiety will naturally decrease in intensity.

CIRCLE TIME QUESTIONS

Ask students to reflect and share their answers to the following questions with the group.

- Have you ever practiced any kind of mindfulness before?
- Why do you think being present in your body and your environment helps with anxiety?
- What about slowing down our thinking would help with some of the other strategies we have learned (such as interrupting the Think-Feel-Do Cycle)?

STORY TIME

Hand out coloring sheets and crayons or markers to younger students while the facilitator reads the story, if desired.

Stop and Smell the Roses

Whenever anyone asked Grant how he was, his answer was, "Busy." Over the years, Grant had learned that keeping busy was the best way for him to be successful. He kept busy at home on the computer, listening to music, calling his friends, and doing chores. He kept busy at school with his classes, after-school clubs and activities, and studying.

And while it was not bad to be busy, Grant's stepfather often asked him things like, "Grant, when are you going to take a break to smell the roses?" To which Grant usually replied, "When the roses help me get everything done!"

Grant was busier this school year than he had ever been. He was trying to make the honor roll, joined three after-school clubs, and recently started taking piano lessons. The more he did, the busier he got. At first, this felt great. He was getting lots of praise from his teachers, earning good grades, and picking up piano quickly. Then, after a few months, things started to change. He felt tired. He was irritated all the time. He started making mistakes. He was worried something was wrong with him. He decided he had to work even harder.

One day, Grant was staying late after school to help paint the set for the upcoming show his drama class was performing. When he walked into the theater, he saw his drama teacher, Ms. Gaffigan, and all his classmates who were acting in the play, sitting in a circle, not talking, with their eyes closed. *That's weird,* Grant thought. *Don't we all have a ton of work to do?*

He approached the circle. Ms. Gaffigan opened her eyes, then motioned for him to take the empty seat. Grant hesitated, then sat down. Ms. Gaffigan began to speak.

"We all lead busy, busy lives. We get up early. We go to bed late. We run from class to class, activity to activity. Sometimes I find myself so tangled up in being busy, that I forget to just *be*. I often think that when I am at my busiest, even though I may be moving quickly, I am not moving mindfully. And when I am not moving my body mindfully, my mind cannot stop moving. And even though I am working day and night, I also find that I make more mistakes because my mind is never in the present—it is always three tasks ahead."

Grant knew she was talking to everyone, but it felt like her message was just for him. She continued.

"One of the most important things we can do in our lives is to be exactly where we are when we are there. Not in the past. Not in the future. In the present. Moment by moment. This will be our goal today. To see what there is to see, hear what there is to hear, smell what there is to smell, and to feel what there is to feel."

It was at this moment that Grant realized that stopping and smelling the roses would, in fact, help him get everything done after all.

DISCUSSION QUESTIONS

- What makes it hard for Grant to stay in the present? Have you ever felt this way?
- Do you agree with Ms. Gaffigan's message about busyness?
- How might being mindful more often help Grant? How might it help you?

SKILL PRACTICE

Ask students how they might apply what Grant learned about mindfulness, giving every student a chance to answer one question. Skill practice can be adapted to allow students to answer in pairs or record their answers on the worksheet.

How might I practice mindfulness:

- When I am stressed about a test?
- If I do not know what to expect in a social situation?
- When I have forgotten to interrupt the Think-Feel-Do Cycle, and my thoughts are stuck in a negative space?
- If I have a competition coming up, and I start to think if I do not win that will mean I have failed?
- When I am upset with my caregivers?
- If I feel left out?
- When it seems like everything is terrible?
- If I have to be in a group with a person I dislike?

ADDITIONAL ACTIVITIES

- Guide the students through a simple grounding exercise. Have them sit quietly. Allowing for time between each prompt, have students notice five things they can see, four things they can feel, three things they can hear, two things they can smell, and one thing they can taste. Let students share how they felt during the exercise.

- Give students the **Mindfulness Techniques Worksheet.** Have them work with a partner to select 2–3 mindfulness techniques they plan to use in the next week. Encourage them to identify any resources or support they need to practice the mindful strategies.

CLOSING CONSIDERATIONS

More than just understanding and interrupting our anxiety, it is important to practice strategies proactively so we can better manage and prevent it. Mindfulness, which connects us to the present and our senses, is one way to do this. We will talk about two more in the coming weeks.

Ask students to summarize the content of the lesson in one sentence. In pairs or groups of three, students may share their answers. If time allows, a few students may share with the whole group. Ask students to try being present and taking things one at a time this week.

"WOULD YOU RATHER?" GAME

Playing the "Would You Rather?" game is a fun and engaging activity for students to develop their critical thinking skills. Students will reflect on their experience, evaluate their options based on their preferences, and reflect on the opinions of others, providing a different perspective and strengthening their sense of connection to one another.

Would You Rather?

Copy and cut out the questions for small groups to discuss, or have students stand in the center of the room and move towards one side or the other to show their vote for either option as the facilitator reads the questions aloud.

- WOULD YOU RATHER TAKE TIME TO BE MINDFUL IN A GROUP OR ALONE?

- WOULD YOU RATHER TRY ONE MINDFULNESS TECHNIQUE AT A TIME OR SEVERAL ALL AT ONCE?

- WOULD YOU RATHER SIT IN A QUIET SPACE OR A CROWDED ROOM?

- WOULD YOU RATHER BE BUSY ALL THE TIME OR TAKE THINGS SLOW?

- WOULD YOU RATHER HAVE SOMEONE REMIND YOU TO STAY PRESENT OR SET A REMINDER FOR YOURSELF?

- WOULD YOU RATHER STAY IN THE PRESENT OR KEEP YOUR THOUGHTS IN THE PAST/FUTURE?

30-MINUTE GROUPS: **ANXIETY MANAGEMENT**

COPING SKILLS – RELAXATION

MIND MAP

On the board, draw a mind map and ask students to consider the meaning of *Coping Skills*.

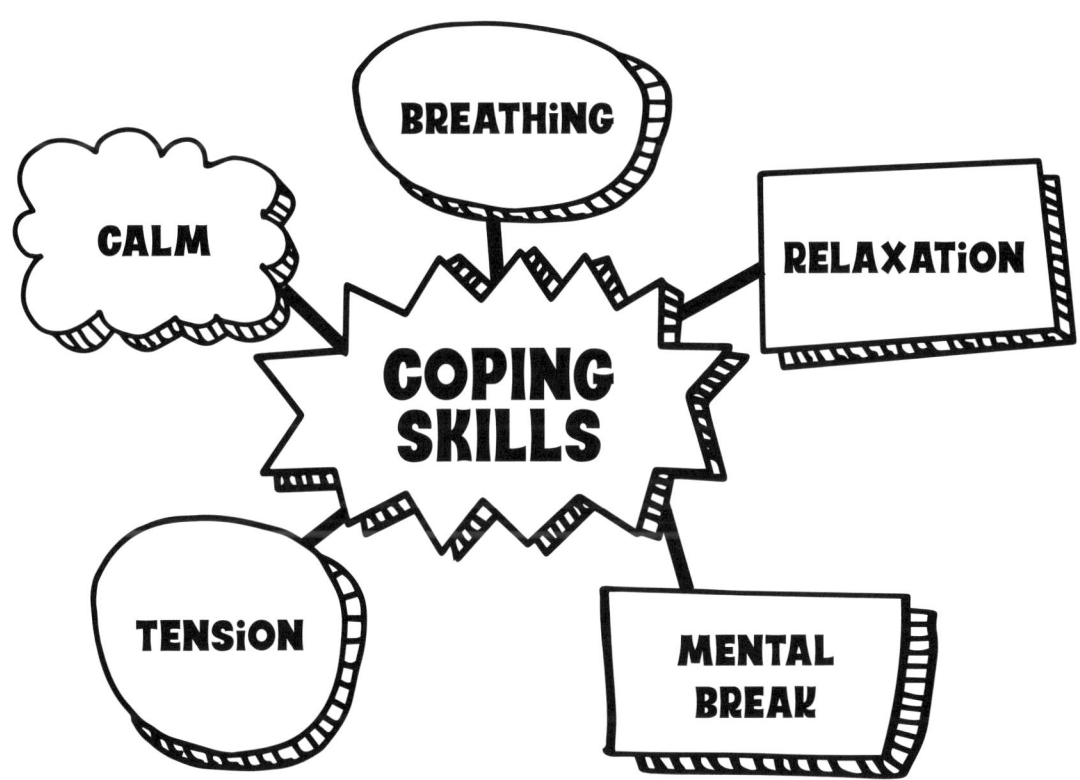

ASCA® STANDARDS

- **B-SMS 7.** Effective coping skills
- **B-SMS 10.** Ability to manage transitions and adapt to change
- **B-SS 3.** Positive relationships with adults to support success
- **B-SS 9.** Social maturity and behaviors appropriate to the situation and environment

DIRECTIONS

- Complete a brief check-in with your students by asking them to share a high and low for the week or by using the weather to represent their emotions.
- Review the Group Expectations.
- Read the Lesson Introduction and ask the Circle Time Questions before reading the Story and asking the Discussion Questions. Students can work in pairs to craft their responses or share with the whole group.
- Complete the Skill Practice, "Would You Rather?" game, and Additional Activities as time allows.
- Be sure to complete the Closing Considerations with each session.

Definitions:

- **Relaxation** is the state of being free from tension and anxiety.

LESSON INTRODUCTION

Anxiety can lead to tense muscles that can cause aches and pain. **Relaxation** is something that we think of when we are taking a break on the weekends or going on a trip. However, there are specific relaxation techniques we can do to help relax tense muscles and ease some of the physical pain anxiety can cause. Relaxation also slows breathing (which we will talk about again next session). This can help reduce symptoms of anxiety such as fast heart rates, high blood pressure, and racing thoughts.

There are several techniques that you can use to achieve relaxation such as stretching, leisurely walks, listening to calming music, taking a bath, etc. Some activities you can do anywhere, such as taking a mini brain vacation.

We will do an example now. Close your eyes and imagine you are at one of your favorite places. Visualize what you see around you. Imagine what you would hear and smell. Pretend that you are engaging in an activity that you would do at your favorite place. Let your body react as if you were in your favorite place. Doing this even for just five minutes can help you relax and reset when you are feeling anxious.

CIRCLE TIME QUESTIONS

Ask students to reflect and share their answers to the following questions with the group.

- Consider the mini brain vacation we just took; how did that feel in your body? Where did you go?
- Where do you feel tension and stress in your body?
- What relaxation techniques have you tried before? What has worked for you and what has not?

STORY TIME

Hand out coloring sheets and crayons or markers to younger students while the facilitator reads the story, if desired.

Relaxation Revelation

Urvi was working on her relaxation skills to help manage her anxiety, but it was not going well. Her school counselor had given her an entire list of ideas for relaxing, but none had worked. Bubble baths made her antsy. She could not stand when her nail polish chipped after a manicure. Whenever she tried to meditate, she just ended up thinking about everything she was not doing.

"What am I doing wrong?" Urvi asked, Ms. Roten, her school counselor during their next conversation. "Why am I so bad at relaxing?"

Ms. Roten smiled.

"Urvi, you are not doing anything wrong. Not everything feels relaxing to everyone. The list is not complete; it is a starting point to give you ideas. However, trying is the most important part. Keep practicing. You will find what helps you become calm and relieves your tension."

Though she had her doubts, Urvi trusted Ms. Roten and did not want to give up yet. She wanted to help her mind and body feel calm. When she got home that night, she looked at her list. Nothing on it seemed like something she wanted to do. She did not want to take a walk. She did not want to drink warm tea. She did not want to read a book. So, she decided to sit and think about the question: *When do I feel the most calm?*

She thought and thought. She wrote down everything that came to her mind. And then she thought some more. Suddenly, it was like a light bulb turned on in her head. It was not on the list, but Urvi knew exactly when she felt calmest. In her dark room, listening to sad, slow music just before bed. The darkness felt like a cozy blanket, and the music helped her connect to her feelings in a way she could not explain.

She shared this during her next meeting with her school counselor.

"Am I weird?" Urvi asked.

"Of course not," Ms. Roten replied. "When we are learning about ourselves, there is nothing weird about it. You can only get more relaxed from here."

DISCUSSION QUESTIONS

- Do you think Urvi was successful in finding what helped her relax? Use the story to support your opinion.
- Have you ever tried something that worked for other people and not you? How did that feel?
- Do you find it easy or difficult to relax? Explain your answer.

SKILL PRACTICE

Ask students how they might apply what Urvi learned about relaxation as a coping skill, giving every student a chance to answer one question. Skill practice can be adapted to allow students to answer in pairs or record their answers on the worksheet.

How might you find a way to relax:

- When it feels like you have too much to do?
- If you are home?
- Before a test at school?
- If you are on vacation?
- Before you try something new?
- When you are with other people?
- When your anxiety feels like it is escalating?
- When your body feels super tense?

ADDITIONAL ACTIVITIES

- Tell the students that progressive relaxation is another strategy that can help reduce the tension that often accompanies anxiety. This is best completed lying down in a quiet space. However, it can be done at your desk too. Take the students through the following Progressive Muscle Relaxation exercise:

    As you are comfortable, close your eyes and take a deep breath. With each of the following muscle groups, hold the body parts tense for 5–10 seconds. Then exhale, breathing deeply as you relax for 15–20 seconds before moving to the next body part. You can do this 1–2 times a day to increase your awareness of the physical symptoms of anxiety, promote relaxation, and reduce pain.

    - *Point your feet and toes.*
    - *Straighten legs and squeeze knees together.*
    - *Flatten stomach toward spine.*
    - *Arch back and draw shoulder blades together.*
    - *Bend hands back at wrists.*
    - *Put palms together and press.*
    - *Raise shoulders up to ears.*
    - *Clench teeth and smile.*
    - *Squeeze eyes shut and wrinkle nose.*
    - *Lift eyebrows up.*

This **Progressive Muscle Relaxation Prompt** is included in the downloadable resources for your convenience.

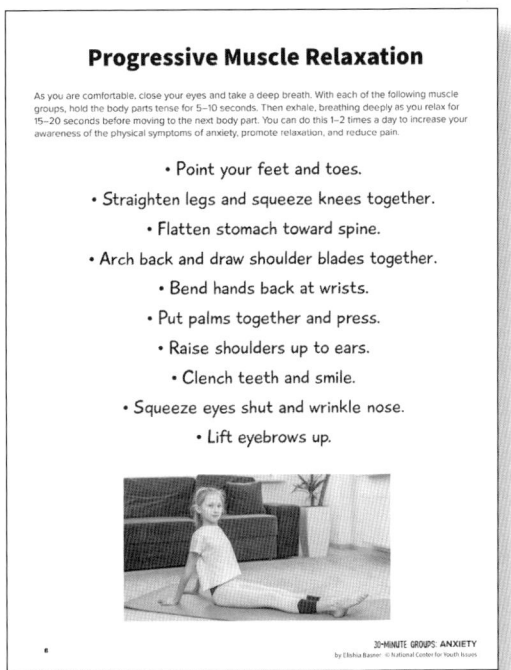

- Have students pair off or work in threes to make a list together of things they would like to try in order to help them relax. Tell them to come up with 5–8 things and each plan to try 1–2 different ones between this session and the next.

CLOSING CONSIDERATIONS

There are tried and true relaxation techniques, but it is also important to make sure you are doing what feels relaxing to you. To do that, you need to try different things. It is okay if something you find relaxing is not relaxing for someone else, and the other way around. Make sure that your relaxing activity does not hurt you, another person, or someone's property. However, finding strategies to relieve tension is extremely important when learning to manage anxiety. Next week, we are going to look at one more coping skill: deep breathing.

Ask students to summarize the content of the lesson in one sentence. In pairs or groups of three, students may share their answers. If time allows, a few students may share with the whole group. Ask students to try an activity or technique this week specifically with the purpose of relaxing.

"WOULD YOU RATHER?" GAME

Playing the "Would You Rather?" game is a fun and engaging activity for students to develop their critical thinking skills. Students will reflect on their experience, evaluate their options based on their preferences, and reflect on the opinions of others, providing a different perspective and strengthening their sense of connection to one another.

WOULD YOU RATHER?

Copy and cut out the questions for small groups to discuss, or have students stand in the center of the room and move towards one side or the other to show their vote for either option as the facilitator reads the questions aloud.

- WOULD YOU RATHER RELAX BY THE BEACH OR IN A MOUNTAIN CABIN?

- WOULD YOU RATHER RELAX BY TAKING A BATH OR SWIMMING IN A POOL?

- WOULD YOU RATHER RELAX WITH OTHER PEOPLE OR BY YOURSELF?

- WOULD YOU RATHER RELAX BY BEING STILL OR DOING AN ACTIVITY?

- WOULD YOU RATHER RELAX BY READING A BOOK OR WATCHING A SHOW YOU LIKE?

- WOULD YOU RATHER RELAX WITH SLOW MUSIC OR UPBEAT MUSIC?

CHAPTER 9
COPING SKILLS – BREATHING

MIND MAP

On the board, draw a mind map and ask students to consider the meaning of *Coping Skills*.

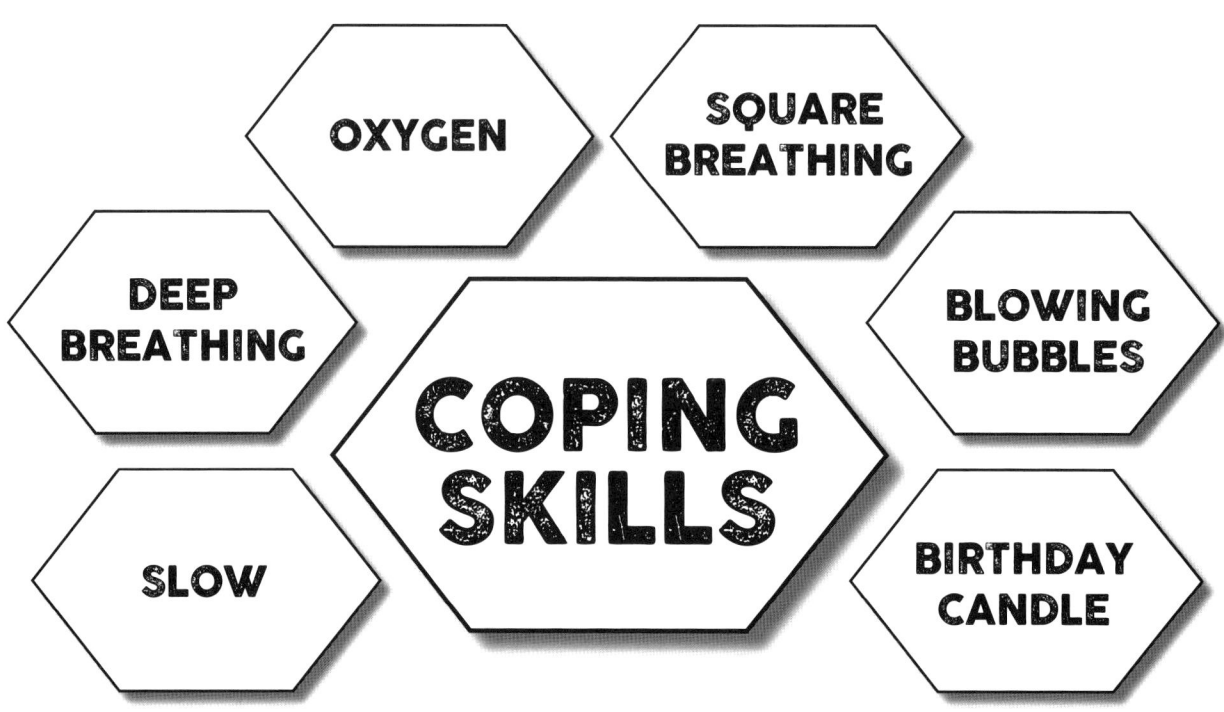

ASCA® STANDARDS

- **B-SMS 7.** Effective coping skills
- **B-SMS 10.** Ability to manage transitions and adapt to change
- **B-SS 2.** Positive, respectful, and supportive relationships with students who are similar to and different from them
- **B-SS 9.** Social maturity and behaviors appropriate to the situation and environment

DIRECTIONS

- Complete a brief check-in with your students by asking them to share a high and low for the week or by using the weather to represent their emotions.
- Review the Group Expectations.
- Read the Lesson Introduction and ask the Circle Time Questions before reading the Story and asking the Discussion Questions. Students can work in pairs to craft their responses or share with the whole group.
- Complete the Skill Practice, "Would You Rather?" game, and Additional Activities as time allows.
- Be sure to complete the Closing Considerations with each session.

Definitions:

- **Deep breathing** is intentionally taking in air through the nose and exhaling through the mouth, using the diaphragm and abdominal muscles. This can help our sympathetic nervous system calm down and reset.

LESSON INTRODUCTION

The last coping strategy we are going to talk about in our group is **breathing**, specifically deep breathing. It is true that we all breathe all the time. However, when we can slow down our breathing, this will not only help us be mindful and relaxed (our other two coping strategies), but can help us be healthier. Deep breathing promotes better oxygen circulation throughout our bodies and signals to our brains that it is safe to relax. Relaxed breathing is slower and deeper than our normal breathing. It happens lower in our belly, or diaphragm, rather than in our chest.

Tips for deep breathing:

- Breathe through your nose instead of your mouth.
- Slow your breathing down. Breathe in for a count of four, pause, and then breathe out to a count of four.
- Breaths should be smooth and steady.
- Deep breathing should happen in your belly. Put one hand on your chest and one on your stomach. The hand on your stomach should be the only one moving.
- Try to practice deep breathing for 5–10 minutes several times a day, especially when you start to feel anxiety increase.

We are going to try ten deep breaths now. I will keep count.

CIRCLE TIME QUESTIONS

Ask students to reflect and share their answers to the following questions with the group.

- What was your experience when we did our deep breaths? How did it feel in your brain and your body?
- Have you ever tried to use breathing to help manage your anxiety before?
- Why do you think breathing is one of the techniques we are practicing in the group?

STORY TIME

Hand out coloring sheets and crayons or markers to younger students while the facilitator reads the story, if desired.

Remember to Breathe

"Remember to breathe!" Austin's aunt called cheerily after him as he left for school.

Austin rolled his eyes. She was always trying to get him to "slow down and breathe" but he had not really seen how it helps yet. He was already breathing all the time, right?

When he got to school, he caught up with his friend Jessica. Austin and Jessica had known each other for a long time. They tried to take as many classes together as they could, and they always tried to partner for group work. Today, they had a presentation in social studies, which was their first class and Austin's favorite subject. It was Jessica's least favorite subject.

They had been working on the presentation for weeks, and Austin felt like they were prepared. They had even planned a big entrance, where they came in from the hallway pretending to be the historical figures who were the subject of their presentation. When it was their turn to present, they went into the hallway. Out of nowhere, Jessica gripped Austin's arm and looked at him with big eyes.

"Austin, I can't do this! My heart is beating so fast. I don't think I'm going to remember my lines. We're going to fail; I just know it!" she whispered.

He could see she was frantic. She was looking around the hallway like someone was chasing her, even though they were the only ones there. Then his aunt's words popped into his head, *Don't forget to breathe!*

Austin put his hand on Jessica's shoulder.

"Jessica, look at me. We've got this. All we have to do is breathe."

Austin started to breathe in through his nose, then out through his mouth. He breathed slow and deep. Jessica started to breathe with him and after a couple of minutes, she was calm again.

"I can do this, right?" she asked.

"We both can. Just breathe."

DISCUSSION QUESTIONS

- What did Austin learn about what deep breathing can do?
- What advice would you give Jessica in the future for a similar situation?
- Have you ever had to help someone else calm down? What did you do?

SKILL PRACTICE

Ask students how they might apply what Austin learned about using breathing to reduce anxiety, giving every student a chance to answer one question. Skill practice can be adapted to allow students to answer in pairs or record on the worksheet.

How might you practice deep breathing:

- When you feel nervous before a test?
- If you are home alone and feeling scared?
- When you are trying to go to sleep?
- If you are trying to be mindful and/or relax?
- When someone says something unkind?
- If you feel your anxiety rising in your body?
- If you need to have an important conversation?

ADDITIONAL ACTIVITIES

If you have time, work through one or more of the following breathing practices. Have students share how each practice felt both in their brain and their body after you complete it.

- **Square Breathing**: As you inhale, draw a horizontal line with your finger in front of you. When you slowly exhale, draw another vertical line down from the end of the horizontal line. Take another slow, deep breath in and draw another horizontal line back in the opposite direction. Finally, as you exhale, draw a vertical line up the corner of the first horizontal line, completing the imaginary square. In addition to the deep breathing, focusing on drawing the square can help distract our brain from what is triggering our anxiety.

- **Birthday Candle**: Pretend that you are holding a cupcake with a lit birthday candle. As you take a deep breath in, make your "birthday wish." Then as you exhale, slowly blow out the birthday candle. Remind students that blowing out the candle too quickly can lead to spitting on the cake. You can pretend that it is a magic candle that will re-light so the students will need to try to blow it out several times before it stays out.

- **Blowing Bubbles**: Give each student a small bottle of bubbles (ex. wedding or party favors). As they try to blow bubbles, remind them to start blowing slowly. Encourage them to take a slow, deep breath and then blow a large bubble as they exhale. They can practice this for several minutes.

CLOSING CONSIDERATIONS

Breathing is not only a wonderful strategy to help manage anxiety on its own, but it is also a way to help us engage with the other two strategies we have learned and practiced, mindfulness and relaxation. One of the best things about breathing is the fact that this strategy is always available to you. You can use it anytime and anywhere.

Ask students to summarize the content of the lesson in one sentence. In pairs or groups of three, students may share their answers. If time allows, a few students may share with the whole group. Ask students to try to take a few minutes every day this week to practice deep breathing and come back next week to share whether it helped and how.

"WOULD YOU RATHER?" GAME

Playing the "Would You Rather?" game is a fun and engaging activity for students to develop their critical thinking skills. Students will reflect on their experience, evaluate their options based on their preferences, and reflect on the opinions of others, providing a different perspective and strengthening their sense of connection to one another.

Would You Rather?

Copy and cut out the questions for small groups to discuss, or have students stand in the center of the room and move towards one side or the other to show their vote for either option as the facilitator reads the questions aloud.

- WOULD YOU RATHER BREATHE WITH QUICK, SHALLOW BREATHS OR DEEP, SLOW ONES?

- WOULD YOU RATHER DEEP BREATHE WHILE USING OTHER COPING SKILLS OR FOCUS ON DEEP BREATHING ONLY?

- WOULD YOU RATHER LET YOUR EMOTIONS CONTROL YOU OR TRY DEEP BREATHING TO SLOW DOWN?

- WOULD YOU RATHER USE A COPING SKILL WHEN SOMEONE UPSETS YOU OR WHEN YOU GET INTO AN ARGUMENT?

- WOULD YOU RATHER HOLD TENSION IN YOUR BODY OR BREATHE IT OUT?

- WOULD YOU RATHER HOLD YOUR BREATH OR DEEP BREATHE WHEN YOU ARE STRESSED?

30-MINUTE GROUPS: ANXIETY MANAGEMENT

> *While we breathe, we will hope.*
> — BARACK OBAMA

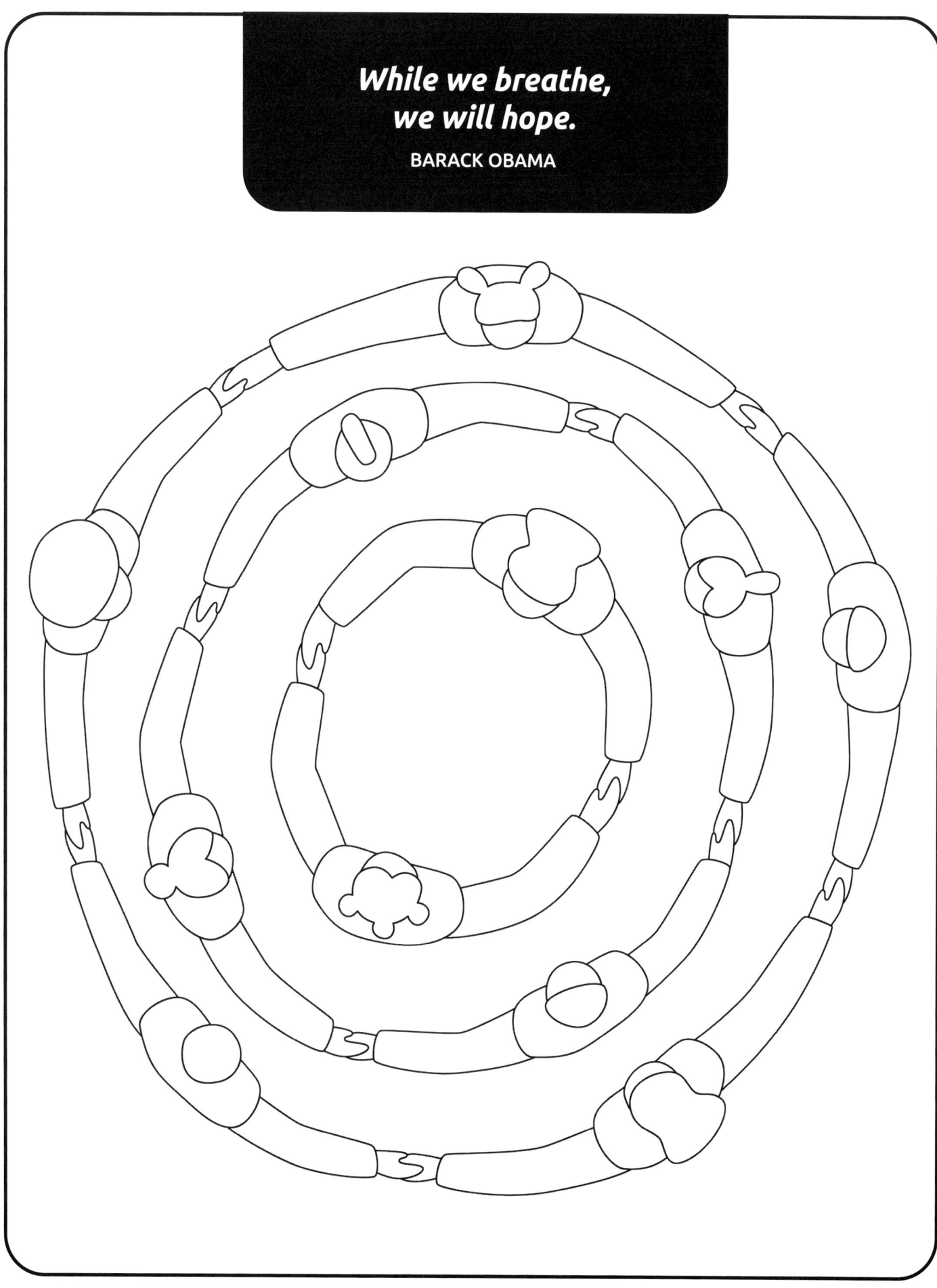

30-MINUTE GROUPS: **ANXIETY MANAGEMENT**

PERSONAL ANXIETY MANAGEMENT PLANNING

MIND MAP

On the board, draw a mind map and ask students to consider the meaning of *Anxiety Management Plan*.

ASCA® STANDARDS

- **B-SMS 1.** Responsibility for self and actions
- **B-SS 9.** Social maturity and behaviors appropriate to the situation and environment
- **B-LS 7.** Long- and short-term academic, career, and social/emotional goals
- **B-SS 1.** Effective oral and written communication skills and listening skills

DIRECTIONS

- Complete a brief check-in with your students by asking them to share a high and low for the week or by using the weather to represent their emotions.
- Review the Group Expectations.
- Read the Lesson Introduction and ask the Circle Time Questions before reading the Story and asking the Discussion Questions. Students can work in pairs to craft their responses or share with the whole group.
- Complete the Skill Practice, "Would You Rather?" game, and Additional Activities as time allows.
- Be sure to complete the Closing Considerations with each session.

Definitions:

- **Fear** is an emotional response to a real or perceived imminent threat.
- **Anticipation** is worry about future real or perceived threats.

LESSON INTRODUCTION

Anxiety is based on both fear and anticipation. Fear is an emotional response to a triggering event. Anticipation is worrying about that potential triggering event before it happens. It can look like fear or worry about how well we will do on a test. Fear or worry about what will happen to a friend or loved one when we are not with them. The anticipation or fear of what others may think of us when we try something new. Fear of not meeting our own or other people's expectations of us. If we can reduce those fears and worries, we reduce the fuel that increases our anxiety.

Imagine that you are at home, and you hear a loud crash. If you do not immediately know what made the crashing sound, you might feel afraid. Could there be someone or something in the house that should not be? Did a tree fall into the house? Is the roof falling in?

There are a lot of possibilities that may create some fear. Until we know what happened, our fear will continue to grow. Once we find out the cause of the crashing sound, then we can take some action and move past the fear. What if you find out that your sibling knocked over a box in the garage? Or that the dog ran into the garbage can? Those explanations are not so scary.

In the same way, if we are feeling anxious about having to speak in front of the class, talking through all the possibilities gives us some knowledge of what might happen. We can explore the positive outcomes as well as the negative ones. Both will give us some knowledge instead of wondering "what if?"

When a person struggles with anxiety and fear, it can be extremely helpful to create a plan for how they will respond to fear when it comes. This is where we will focus today, using all the knowledge we have gained in our time together.

CIRCLE TIME QUESTIONS

Ask students to reflect and share their answers to the following questions with the group.

- After all our small group lessons, what have you learned about the way anxiety and fear play a role in your life?
- Have you noticed any changes in your ability to manage your anxiety in the last several weeks? What kinds of changes?
- When have you created a plan to help prepare for something before? How did it go?

STORY TIME

Hand out coloring sheets and crayons or markers to younger students while the facilitator reads the story, if desired.

Fear with a Plan

Cameron was afraid of thunderstorms. He had been his whole life. Everyone had tried to convince him that he did not need to be afraid—his parents, his siblings, his friends. However, Cameron could not be convinced. Thunderstorms were terrifying and that was that.

One week, there was a huge thunderstorm warning. Phones were buzzing, the sky was dark, and sirens were going off in the community. He had never had to be at school for a bad storm before. He heard teachers talking about using those storm warning drills they had practiced before. Going home would not be an option because no one was allowed to be on the roads.

Cameron's stomach was tied in knots and so were his thoughts. How was he going to manage this? He did the only thing he could think of: before they were told to start the safety drill procedures, he asked to talk to the school counselor, Ms. Pike. When he got to Ms. Pike's office, his fear was so big, that he could barely tell her what was wrong. However, after a few deep breaths, he told her about his fear.

Ms. Pike did not seem surprised at all.

"Lots of people are afraid of thunderstorms. All we need is a plan," she said.

And so, while the sky got darker and darker, Ms. Pike and Cameron came up with a plan for what he was going to do when the storm started. They made a plan for how he would handle his emotions and how he would handle the discomfort in his body. They talked about what to do when it felt like too much, and how to help himself calm down before his fear took over.

By the end, Cameron did not love thunderstorms, but he felt more ready than he ever had.

DISCUSSION QUESTIONS

- Why did Ms. Pike and Cameron's plan have so much power to help?
- What skills did Cameron use even before he had a plan?
- What do you think of the idea that fear and anxiety do not go away, we just get better at managing them?

SKILL PRACTICE

Ask students how they might apply what Cameron learned about making a plan to handle his fear, giving every student a chance to answer one question. Skill practice can be adapted to allow students to answer in pairs or record their answers on the worksheet.

- Instead of the typical skills practice, students should use this time to complete their **My Personal Safety Plan Worksheet.**
- If needed or helpful, students can work in pairs or threes to help one another.
- When they are done, offer students the opportunity to share.

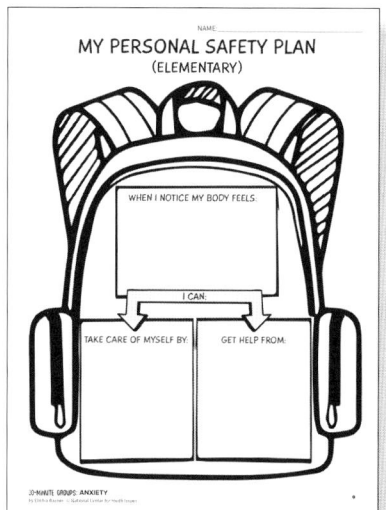
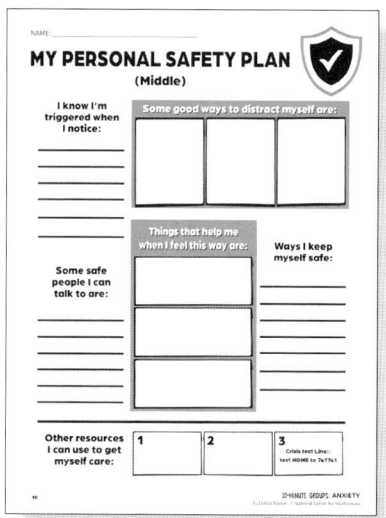

ADDITIONAL ACTIVITIES

- Ask students to choose at least one "go-to" coping skill they will use to reduce their anxiety at school and another coping skill they can use at home. Probe the students to identify any materials or resources they will need to successfully use their coping skills.
- Practice how the students can tell their teacher and/or caregivers about their new coping skills and ask for permission to use them. Pair the students off and let them role-play with one another using their Personal Safety Plan worksheets.

CLOSING CONSIDERATIONS

Anxiety and fear are linked. When they show up together, we have reactions in our brains and bodies. We might have irrational thoughts or draw faulty conclusions. It might be difficult to stay calm. However, if we know what triggers our anxiety, we can make a plan for it. This is how we begin to successfully manage our anxiety instead of allowing our anxiety to manage us. It does not disappear, but when we understand ourselves and can respond to our anxiety effectively, we realize our problems are not as big as we thought.

Ask students to summarize the content of the lesson in one sentence. In pairs or groups of three, students may share their answers. If time allows, a few students may share with the whole group. Ask the students to try and use their plan this week. If this is the last session, be sure the students complete the Post-Group Survey and thank them for their engagement and participation.

"WOULD YOU RATHER?" GAME

Playing the "Would You Rather?" game is a fun and engaging activity for students to develop their critical thinking skills. Students will reflect on their experience, evaluate their options based on their preferences, and reflect on the opinions of others, providing a different perspective and strengthening their sense of connection to one another.

WOULD YOU RATHER?

Copy and cut out the questions for small groups to discuss, or have students stand in the center of the room and move towards one side or the other to show their vote for either option as the facilitator reads the questions aloud.

- WOULD YOU RATHER PLAN FOR SOMETHING OR FIGURE IT OUT IN THE MOMENT?

- WOULD YOU RATHER LIVE IN FEAR OR BE ABLE TO FACE LIFE HEAD-ON?

- WOULD YOU RATHER FEEL HELPLESS OR UNDERSTAND HOW TO HELP YOURSELF?

- WOULD YOU RATHER EXPERIENCE FIGHT, FLIGHT, FREEZE, AND FAWN RESPONSES OR TAKE SOME CONTROL OF YOUR ACTIONS?

- WOULD YOU RATHER TELL YOUR CAREGIVERS ABOUT YOUR COPING SKILLS OR KEEP THEM TO YOURSELF?

- WOULD YOU RATHER PICK A GO-TO COPING SKILL OR DECIDE AS YOU NEED IT?

30-MINUTE GROUPS: ANXIETY MANAGEMENT

Final Group Session

LAST SESSION:
Directions & Overview

This final session is recommended, but optional. You may conclude the group during the final lesson topic if time does not permit this final session.

Directions: This final session is not as structured as the previous lessons to allow students to reflect on what they have learned, process their feelings about the group's conclusion, and celebrate their growth. Review the lessons learned throughout the group sessions:

- Some anxiety is a normal part of life.
- When anxiety keeps us from taking part in our regular activities, we may be experiencing what is considered high levels of anxiety, levels that require more support and intervention, which could include counseling and medical support. It is okay to have these feelings and to reach out to trusted adults for help and support when feeling overwhelmed.
- Anxiety is a physiological response to a perceived threat in the environment. That response prepares the body to protect itself from danger by fighting, fleeing, fawning, or not moving at all. This acute stress response is more commonly known as the Fight, Flight, Freeze, or Fawn response.
- The body has four types of responses to that release of hormones and the amygdala's call for protection:
  - Fight: face the danger and fight the threat aggressively.
  - Flight: run away from the threat to try and save yourself.
  - Freeze: do not move or hide in hopes of being ignored until the threat passes.
  - Fawn: submit to or bargain with the threat in hopes of avoiding conflict.
- When we know what anxiety looks like we can intervene and use positive coping skills to keep it from escalating and getting worse. Anxiety can reveal itself physically, emotionally, and behaviorally.
- There is a relationship between our thoughts, feelings, and behaviors. We call this the Think-Feel-Do Cycle.
- One of the ways that we can manage our anxiety is to interrupt the Think-Feel-Do Cycle. When we change our anxiety-inducing thoughts, it will help us to reduce our anxious behaviors.
- There are activities that we can use to help us slow down and pay more attention to thoughts, feelings, and behaviors that often lead to anxiety. These coping skills will help us feel more in control of ourselves when feeling anxious or overwhelmed.

Encourage the students to share how their learning has made a difference in their own journeys to better manage their anxiety. There are several activities that you can use to facilitate this closing discussion, such as:

- **Individual Reflection**: Ask the students to share one lesson, activity, or skill that has helped them to better manage their anxiety. It is important to emphasize the students' agency and control over handling their anxious feelings.

- **Success Stories**: Allow students to share a time when they have used the lessons, activities, and/or skills to better manage their anxiety.

- **Peer Observation**: Ask students to share something they have observed a fellow group member do to better manage their anxiety. This could be both in the group meeting or outside of group time.

- **Peer Teaching**: Ask students to share something they have learned from another group member that has helped them to better manage their own anxiety.

- **Anxiety-Busting Superhero**: In the first session, students may have introduced themselves as a superhero identity. Revisit this activity, asking students to describe themselves now as Anxiety-Busting Superheroes with special superpowers they can use to help get rid of anxiety. Allow them to come up with creative names, color capes or costumes that reflect their superpowers, etc., and share them with the group.

Post-Group Expectations: Many students will have grown accustomed to meeting with you and will need reassurance about what support will be available after the group's conclusion. Be sure to review the protocol for meeting with you once the group has concluded.

Pre- and Post-Group Survey: If you administered a Pre-Group Survey, this would be a good time to conduct a Post-Group Survey to help prepare the students to reflect on their individual growth. If you decided to modify the questions and/or presentation of the Pre-Group Survey, you should administer the Post-Group Survey using the same questions, method, and presentation model to best measure the growth for each student. Depending on the grade level of the students in your group, you may select 3–5 questions from the Pre- and Post-Group Survey instead of having them complete the full assessment.

Certificate of Completion: Present each student with their own Certificate of Completion. You can have as much or as little fanfare around this experience as you would like. Playing a song and asking students to stand and clap for their peers can create lasting memories for the participants.

Group Completion Letter: Give each student their Group Completion Letter to share with their caregiver, notifying them that the group has officially ended.

Group Conclusion: Ask each student to share what, if anything, this group has meant to them. Model this activity by sharing your experience as the group's facilitator. It may also be helpful to include the following in your wrap-up discussion:

- Thank the students for their participation.

- Remind students that anxiety will not just disappear; however, when they use the information and skills that they have learned, they will be able to manage it better.

- Explain what the students should do if they need some additional support. Normalize needing a follow-up individual check-in. Identify other adults they can go to for support.

- Prompt the students to remember the Group Norm not to repeat what is said during the group meeting to anyone outside of the group.

Note to Facilitators: If your district allows it, a group meal is often a fun experience for the students. If you cannot purchase a meal within the district budget, perhaps students could bring their own lunch. Be sure to have caregiving permission and be familiar with students' allergies before providing food.

SMALL GROUP ACTION PLAN GUIDE

GRADE LEVEL
The curriculum is ideal for 2nd through 8th grade students.

GROUP TOPICS
- Is Anxiety Normal?
- Your Brain on Anxiety
- Your Body on Anxiety
- Types of Anxiety
- The Think-Feel-Do Cycle
- Interrupting the Think-Feel-Do Cycle
- Coping Skills – Mindfulness
- Coping Skills - Relaxation
- Coping Skills – Breathing
- Personal Anxiety Management Planning

10-12 Group Sessions — 30 MIN

CURRICULUM & MATERIALS

Curriculum:
Use this 30-Minute Groups: Anxiety Management workbook to facilitate your groups.

Materials:
Copies of surveys, coloring sheets, worksheets, and "Would You Rather?" game. Crayons, pencils, markers, scratch paper, and a whiteboard/chalkboard/smartboard, if available.

ASCA® STUDENT BEHAVIOR STANDARDS — 14

- B-LS 1
- B-LS 2
- B-LS 7
- B-SMS 1
- B-SMS 2
- B-SMS 6
- B-SMS 7
- B-SMS 10
- B-SS 1
- B-SS 2
- B-SS 3
- B-SS 4
- B-SS 8
- B-SS 9

NUMBER OF STUDENTS AFFECTED
Group counseling is ideal for 6–8 students, and fewer students if the goals are related to behavioral issues. However, the lessons for each session can be adapted for classroom lessons as well.

PERCEPTION DATA

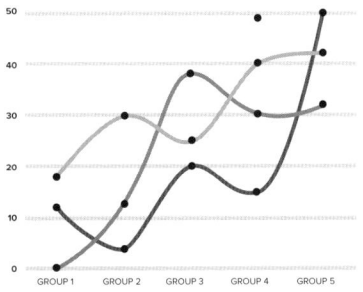

Use Anxiety survey data to create a visual representation of their progress using their pre- and post-data.

OUTCOME DATA

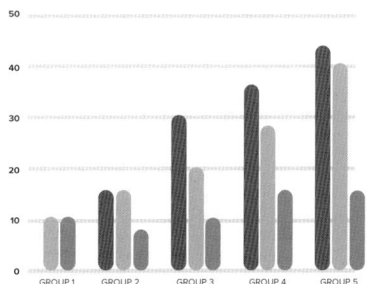

Use achievement, attendance, and behavior data to measure the progress of your students. Compare Pre- and Post-Group Surveys to determine the impact of the group lessons on students.

30-MINUTE GROUPS: ANXIETY MANAGEMENT

ANXIETY MANAGEMENT GROUP PERMISSION FORM

Greetings, Caregivers of: _____,

Our counseling department offers various services, including class lessons, groups, and individual sessions with students. We are inviting your student to attend an Anxiety Management Group. There are lots of reasons we invite students to attend groups. We invite students who might need help connecting with their peers, help with skills to manage conflict or big emotions, to improve their grades, or simply because we think their involvement will allow them to be more successful in their educational journey. Your student is not in trouble, and this group is meant to be a positive time for all attendees.

This group will focus on building skills related to understanding and normalizing anxiety, its connection to the body, different types of anxiety, and, perhaps most importantly, coping skills to help manage anxiety when it occurs.

We will meet for approximately thirty minutes during the school day _____ times per week beginning the week of _____. I will work with your child's teacher to select an appropriate time that minimizes interruptions to their learning. When the students have completed all the group sessions, they will receive a Certificate of Completion.

I am excited to work with your child! Please feel free to contact me with any questions or concerns.

Warm Regards,

Please complete and return by: _____

Student's Name: _____

Teacher's Name: _____

☐ YES, I agree to allow my child to attend the Anxiety Management Group.

☐ NO, I do NOT agree to allow my child to attend the Anxiety Management Group.

_____
Signature of Caregiver

ANXIETY MANAGEMENT GROUP EXPECTATIONS

CONFIDENTIALITY

We know that some things are private, and not everyone needs to know about them. What is shared in the group should stay in the group, and not be repeated to anyone outside the group. However, because we are a group, we cannot promise that everyone will keep your secrets, so please be mindful of what you share with the group. If you have a major concern, you can always share it with me privately before or after the group meeting. If you share that you plan to hurt yourself or someone else, or that someone is hurting you, I will have to notify the appropriate adults to protect you.

LISTEN CAREFULLY

To listen is more than to hear. When others are speaking, we all must do our best to focus on what others say with all of our senses, refrain from interrupting, and keep our minds in the present without trying to decide what we will say next.

SHOW EVERYONE RESPECT

We show our respect for the others in our group by giving our full attention to the speaker, giving everyone a chance to talk in each group, and being safe people for one another. This means responding with curiosity, not criticism, when we think, look, or act differently than another person. This also means responding with kindness if conflict or disagreement occurs.

PARTICIPATE IN OUR GROUP ACTIVITIES

We are here to work together, so it is important that each one of us is doing our part to participate and engage. This will help us deepen our understanding of the topic, ourselves, and one another, which will enrich our learning and growth.

CREATE YOUR OWN

_____

_____

_____

_____

Group Attendance Form

Group:_____ Day/Time:_____

	1	2	3	4	5	6	7	8	9	10	11	12
DATE												
	☐	☐	☐	☐	☐	☐	☐	☐	☐	☐	☐	☐
	☐	☐	☐	☐	☐	☐	☐	☐	☐	☐	☐	☐
	☐	☐	☐	☐	☐	☐	☐	☐	☐	☐	☐	☐
	☐	☐	☐	☐	☐	☐	☐	☐	☐	☐	☐	☐
	☐	☐	☐	☐	☐	☐	☐	☐	☐	☐	☐	☐
	☐	☐	☐	☐	☐	☐	☐	☐	☐	☐	☐	☐
	☐	☐	☐	☐	☐	☐	☐	☐	☐	☐	☐	☐

SESSION 1

SESSION 2

SESSION 3

SESSION 4

SESSION 5

SESSION 6

SESSION 7

SESSION 8

SESSION 9

SESSION 10

SESSION 11

SESSION 12

Group Attendance Form (Example)

Group: 5th Grade Lunch   **Day/Time:** Thursday @ 12:30

	1	2	3	4	5	6	7	8	9	10	11	12
DATE	3/2	3/9	3/16	3/23								
Jane/Ms. W's Class	X	X	X	X	X	X	X	X	X	X	X	X
George/Mr. Day's Class	X	X		X	X	X	X	X	X	X	X	X
Sami/Ms. Smith's Class	X	X	X	X	X	X	X	X	X	X	X	X
John/Ms. Lee's Class	X		X	X	X	X	X	X	X	X	X	X
Malik/Ms. Lee's Class	X	X	X		X	X		X	X	X	X	X
Prishna/Ms. Smith's Class	X	X	X	X	X	X	X	X		X	X	X

SESSION 1	Intro/Surveys/Group Rules and Norms/Discussed expectations/Played game.
SESSION 2	Is Anxiety Normal?
SESSION 3	Your Brain on Anxiety
SESSION 4	Your Body on Anxiety
SESSION 5	Types of Anxiety
SESSION 6	The Think-Feel-Do Cycle
SESSION 7	Interrupting the Think-Feel-Do Cycle
SESSION 8	Coping Skills – Mindfulness
SESSION 9	Coping Skills – Relaxation
SESSION 10	Coping Skills – Breathing
SESSION 11	Personal Anxiety Management Planning
SESSION 12	Check-ins/Post-Group Survey/Process group experience & Certificates awarded.

Pre- and Post- Group Survey

My name is: _____   Total Score:_____

Date: _____

Directions: Check the answer to each question below. If you do not know the answer, take your best guess.

1. Anxiety is a normal part of life.

    ❏ True   ❏ False

2. Anxiety is our body's way of letting us know that we may not be safe or that we care a lot about something.

    ❏ True   ❏ False

3. If we feel high levels of worry that cause us physical and mental distress, and these feelings impact what we want to do or need to do, we may need:

    A. Medical support
    B. To ignore it until it goes away
    C. To talk to a counselor
    D. A and C

4. Anxiety is your body's response to a real and immediate threat.

    ❏ True   ❏ False

5. The part of your brain that controls the anxiety you feel is called the:

    A. Cerebrum
    B. Brain Stem
    C. Amygdala
    D. Not sure

6. Fight, Flight, Freeze, and Fawn are the four responses that play a role in anxiety.

    ❏ True   ❏ False

7. Name one physical, one emotional, and one behavioral symptom of anxiety that you experience.

    Physical:_____

    Emotional: _____

    Behavioral: _____

8. What is the Think-Feel-Do Cycle?

   _____

   _____

   _____

9. Where is the best place to interrupt the Think-Feel-Do cycle to reduce anxiety?

   A. Think
   B. Feel
   C. Do

10. Describe two coping skills you can use to help manage your anxiety.

    Coping Skill 1: _____

    Coping Skill 2: _____

Anything else you would like to share about the group? Write it below.

_____

_____

_____

Pre- and Post- Group Survey Answer Key

1. Anxiety is a normal part of life.

   True

2. Anxiety is our body's way of letting us know that we may not be safe or that we care a lot about something.

   True

3. If we feel high levels of worry that cause us physical and mental distress, and these feelings impact what we want to do or need to do, we may need:

   D. A and C (Medical support and to talk to a counselor)

4. Anxiety is your body's response to a real and immediate threat.

   False

5. The part of your brain that controls the anxiety you feel is called the:

   C. Amygdala

6. Fight, Flight, Freeze, and Fawn are the four responses that play a role in anxiety.

   True. The Fight, Flight, Freeze, Fawn response is our body's reaction to the amygdala's release of hormones sending a message that we are in danger and need to seek safety. There are four typical responses that our bodies will take to protect us. This is an automatic process that starts once the amygdala detects a threat to our physical, emotional, or social safety.

7. Name one physical, one emotional, and one behavioral symptom of anxiety that you experience.

   Answer: There are numerous possible answers here. Make sure students are aware of and can differentiate between the three ways that anxiety can show up in their bodies.

8. What is the Think-Feel-Do Cycle?

   Answer: The relationship between our thoughts, feelings, and behaviors. Our feelings and behaviors are impacted by the thoughts that we have. If we can change our thoughts, we can often change our feelings and then our behaviors.

9. Where is the best place to interrupt the Think-Feel-Do cycle to reduce anxiety?

   A. Think

10. Describe two coping skills you can use to help manage your anxiety.

    Answer: There are multiple possible answers. Be sure students have identified appropriate and healthy coping skills that will give them better control over their anxiety.

Post-Group Survey Results
Anxiety Management Group Data

GROUP GOAL:

STUDENT STATEMENTS:

Achievement
____% of participants (____ out of ____) increased their academic achievement following group intervention

____%

Attendance
____% of participants (____ out of ____) increased their attendance following group intervention

____%

Behavior
____% of participants (____ out of ____) decreased behavior referrals following group intervention

____%

STUDENTS ATTENDED

NUMBER OF SESSIONS

OVERALL IMPROVEMENT

(See Formula Bottom Page)

Student	Pre-Intervention Assessment Score	Post-Intervention Assessment Score	Percent Increase of Knowledge Gained ((Post Score - Pre Score) / Pre Score) x 100 = Percent Increase
1.			
2.			
3.			
4.			
5.			
6.			
7.			
8.			
TOTAL			

OVERALL IMPROVEMENT FORMULA

$$\left(\frac{\text{Post-Group Total - Pre-Group Total}}{\text{Pre-Group Total}}\right) \times 100$$

Post-Group Survey Results (Example)
Anxiety Management Group Data

GROUP GOAL:

Increase attendance by 10% for a group of 7 students who have missed more than 5 days of school due to anxiety.

STUDENT STATEMENTS:

"Now that I understand what anxiety is, it is not so scary anymore."

"I have learned how to keep my feeling brain from taking over by practicing coping skills."

"I know who I can talk to when I start to feel worried and anxious."

Achievement
__57__% of participants (__4__ out of __7__) increased their academic achievement following group intervention

57%

Attendance
__71__% of participants (__5__ out of __7__) increased their attendance following group intervention

71%

Behavior
__57__% of participants (__4__ out of __7__) decreased behavior referrals following group intervention

57%

STUDENTS ATTENDED: 7

NUMBER OF SESSIONS: 12

OVERALL IMPROVEMENT: 216.6%
(See Formula Bottom Page)

Student	Pre-Intervention Assessment Score	Post-Intervention Assessment Score	Percent Increase of Knowledge Gained ((Post Score - Pre Score) / Pre Score) x 100 = Percent Increase
1. Alix	3 out of 10 (30%)	8 out of 10 (80%)	167% increase
2. Matthew	2 out of 10 (20%)	7 out of 10 (70%)	250% increase
3. Kayden	3 out of 10 (30%)	9 out of 10 (90%)	200% increase
4. Gannon	1 out of 10 (10%)	7 out of 10 (70%)	600% increase
5. Emily	2 out of 10 (20%)	8 out of 10 (80%)	300% increase
6. AJ	3 out of 10 (30%)	8 out of 10 (80%)	167% increase
7. Trinity	4 out of 10 (20%)	10 out of 10 (100%)	150% increase
8.			
TOTAL	18	57	216.6% increase

OVERALL IMPROVEMENT FORMULA AND CALCULATION

$$\left(\frac{\text{Post-Group Total} - \text{Pre-Group Total}}{\text{Pre-Group Total}}\right) \times 100$$

$$\left(\frac{57-18}{18}\right) \times 100 \qquad (2.166) \times 100 = 216.6\%$$

30-MINUTE GROUPS

CERTIFICATE OF COMPLETION

This Certificate is Presented to:

_____

For Participating in the **Anxiety Management Group!**

Facilitator: _____

NiCE JOB!

ANXIETY MANAGEMENT GROUP COMPLETION LETTER

Date:_____

Hello!

Today was the final session in our Anxiety Management Group, and we wanted to let you know that your student has been presented with a Certificate of Completion. Over our time together, we have reviewed the following topics:

- Is Anxiety Normal?
- Your Brain on Anxiety
- Your Body on Anxiety
- Types of Anxiety
- The Think-Feel-Do Cycle
- Interrupting the Think-Feel-Do Cycle
- Coping Skills – Mindfulness
- Coping Skills - Relaxation
- Coping Skills – Breathing
- Personal Anxiety Management Planning

I am still available to your student as needed in the future. However, we will no longer be meeting every week. Please feel free to contact me with any questions or concerns.

I am so proud of your student and excited they were able to attend. Thank you so much for allowing them to participate in our Anxiety Management Group!

Warm regards,

_____

School Counselor

REFERENCES

American School Counselor Association. "Mindsets & Behaviors for Student Success: K-12 College- and Career-Readiness Standards for Every Student." American School Counselor Association. https://www.schoolcounselor.org/getmedia/7428a787-a452-4abb-afec-d78ec77870cd/Mindsets-Behaviors.pdf Accessed June 30, 2024.

Bagwell, Leigh. *15-Minute Focus: Anxiety*. National Center for Youth Issues, 2020.

Bagwell, Leigh. *15-Minute Focus: Anxiety Workbook*. National Center for Youth Issues, 2024.

THE RESOURCES IN THIS BOOK ARE AVAILABLE FOR YOU AS A DIGITAL DOWNLOAD!

Please visit **ncyi.org/downloadable-resources** to access the downloadable resources.

Enter the code below to unlock the resources:

ANXIETY562

ABOUT THE AUTHOR

Dr. Leigh Bagwell is a member of the School Counseling Core Faculty in the School of Social and Behavioral Sciences at Capella University. Bagwell joined Capella in the spring of 2022 shortly after completing her doctorate in Counselor Education and Supervision from the University of Tennessee. She began her career as an elementary and middle school counselor before moving to leadership and supervisory roles in school counseling for preK-12 education in both urban and suburban school districts then ultimately serving as the Director of School Counseling Services for the Tennessee Department of Education. As a school counseling educator and leader, her mission is to provide school counselors and administrators with the training and resources needed to deliver high quality, student driven, data informed comprehensive school counseling programs to all students. She believes when school counselors and school leaders work together to all students have access to the opportunities and supports they need to successfully move through their elementary, secondary, and postsecondary education into their chosen career.

In addition to her work in Tennessee, Bagwell partners with school counselors and school counseling leaders throughout the country using her experiences and knowledge to build their capacity to more effectively serve students. She has authored multiple books in the *15 Minute Focus Series: Self-Harm and Self-Injury: When Emotional Pain Becomes Physical* and *Anxiety: Worry, Stress, and Fear* and an accompanying workbook, along with *30-Minute Groups: Anxiety Management*. Leigh has also served as a consultant on several SEL children's books. She has conducted research on mental health supports for students and families and is a consultant with an international organization developing tools and materials that help school counselors deliver effective school counseling programs to all students. Dr. Bagwell's hope is to equip and empower school counselors to use their unique knowledge and skills to advocate and support all students to reach their potential and achieve their

A Brief Look at Leigh's Workshop Sessions

Support Students Struggling with Anxiety and Stress

Anxiety and stress can cause students to feel isolated and overwhelmed, preventing them from learning in the classroom. When students experience anxiety and stress, they need help navigating through it. Rather than tell our students not to worry, our job as educators is to recognize when students are experiencing anxiety and get them the support they need. During this session we will discuss the physiology of anxiety, signs that a student may be in distress, and specific interventions educators can employ to support their students. We will also highlight steps schools can take to prevent an anxious and stressful learning environment. Working together, educators can become powerful advocates for students struggling with anxiety so that they can thrive in the classroom and in life.

MTSS and School Counseling: Maximizing Supports for Student Success

School counselors work to provide data-driven, evidence-based school counseling programs to impact student achievement, social and personal competencies, and college and career readiness. Multi-Tiered Systems of Support (MTSS) is a research-based framework for addressing student needs through effective prevention and intervention strategies. MTSS has been successfully applied to both academic skills and the positive behavior of all students. Traditionally, school counselors have played an important role in these efforts to advocate and serve students; however, the comprehensive school counseling program (CSCP) has not always been identified as a support for the MTSS model. What if school counselors could align their CSCP to the MTSS framework? Let's explore how connecting these two models will help maximize the effectiveness and efficiency of school counselors, provide more meaningful support to students, and advocate for the many ways that school counselors impact student growth, development, and success.

Social and Emotional Learning

Our emotions and relationships affect how and what we learn and how we use what we learn in school, work, family, and community contexts. As many schools and districts integrate social and emotional learning frameworks into their classroom instruction, services provided by student support staff can be especially effective in promoting the school success of children who have social, emotional, and mental health problems that interfere with learning. During this session participants will discuss the specific role of school counselors, school social workers, school psychologists, school nurses and other student support professionals in supporting the social and emotional learning initiatives that lead to student success.

Integrating Social and Emotional Learning with Career Development to Prepare College and Career Ready Students.

When preparing students for success in postsecondary education and the workforce it is important that they have academic and content knowledge and training. College and career readiness begins with early exposure and awareness to a broad range of career fields and employability skills. It also includes helping students connect what they are learning in the classroom to their dreams and future career goals. Another important component of college and career readiness is social and emotional development. Self-awareness, self-management and interpersonal skills are critical to students' transition to postsecondary and the workforce.

College and career readiness continues to focus on the development and refinement of both academic and social emotional skills. It also broadens the scope from just knowing about different careers to exploring the high demand opportunities in their communities, aligning personal interests and aptitudes to career fields, and identifying specific pathways to move successfully from secondary to postsecondary to the workforce. These skills will not only prepare them for success in the workplace, but also success in both secondary and postsecondary education.

Because school counseling programs integrate academic preparation, social and emotional development with college and career readiness, school counselors are uniquely positioned to lead this important work. It begins by ensuring that school counselors have strategies and practices that will deepen their students' understanding of the world of work and connect it to their school and life experiences. School counselors will increase their capacity to provide high quality school counseling services and support students as they move along their chosen pathways to and through secondary and postsecondary education and on to the workforce.

College and Career Readiness: K(indergarten) to J(ob) K-12 Session

What does a successful student look like? What are the skills, knowledge, and experiences our students need to transition effectively from education and training to the workforce? Preparing today's students for tomorrow's workforce goes beyond the traditional career speakers and "careers on wheels" of days past. More than half of our students will pursue a career that has not been developed yet. College and career readiness begins with early exposure and awareness to a broad range of career fields and employability skills. These skills will not only prepare them for success in the workplace, but also success in both secondary and postsecondary education. When students transition from elementary schools to middle and high schools, they also progress from career awareness to career exploration and planning. College and career readiness continues to focus on the development and refinement of employability skills. It also broadens the scope from just knowing about different careers to exploring the high demand opportunities in their communities, aligning personal interests and aptitudes to career fields, and identifying specific pathways to move successfully from secondary to postsecondary to the workforce.

Using school counseling standards as the foundation, we will discuss the profile of a college and career ready student. Participants will leave with specific school counseling strategies and practices that will deepen their students' understanding of the world of work and connect it to their school experience. School counselors will increase their capacity to provide high quality advising and support students as they move along their chosen pathways to and through secondary and postsecondary education and on to the workforce.

ncyionline.org/speakers

ALSO AVAILABLE FROM LEIGH

15-Minute Focus: Self-Harm and Self-Injury *When Emotional Pain Becomes Physical*

Bagwell offers an in-depth look at the who, what, and why of self-harm; more accurately called nonsuicidal self-injury (NSSI).

This book features stories from students as they explain NSSI from their experiences, giving adults an inside look into the lives of those who struggle with this behavior.

15-Minute Focus: Anxiety
Worry, Stress, and Fear

In this book, Bagwell explains the physiological progression from a trigger to a full-blown anxiety attack, and provides a variety of prevention and intervention strategies for school counselors, educators, and administrators.

15-Minute Focus: Anxiety Workbook
Tips and Strategies to Manage Anxiety, Build Resilience, and Foster Emotional Well-Being

Filled with age-appropriate examples, practical resources, and interactive exercises, in this workbook you will discover knowledge and tools to demystify anxiety, navigate the "why," become an effective advocate, and empower students with coping skills.

30-MINUTE GROUPS

Scan here for more 30-MINUTE GROUPS RESOURCES

BONUS! Includes Downloadable Resources and Templates!

30MinuteGroups.com

30-Minute Groups is a new curriculum series that aims to help school counselors and educators navigate three main challenges they encounter when attempting to start a small group:

- Workload Demands to manage the number of students for whom they are responsible
- No Prep Time to create lessons and activities for small group sessions
- Budget Constraints for ongoing training

The strategic design allows students to empathize, connect with others, and translate their new knowledge into practice. The American School Counselor Association (ASCA®)-aligned curriculum contains an introductory lesson, ten core topical lessons, and a completion session. Practical and applicable, the activities provided are suitable for small and large group instruction and require no additional materials!

 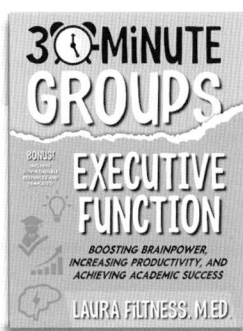  

   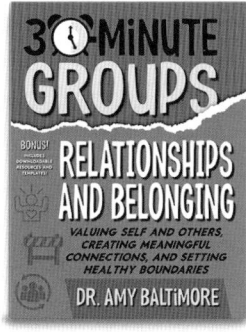 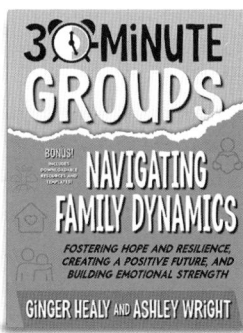

Visit 30MinuteGroups.com for our latest additions to the series!

About NCYI

National Center for Youth Issues provides educational resources, training, and support programs to foster the healthy social, emotional, and physical development of children and youth. Since our founding in 1981, NCYI has established a reputation as one of the country's leading providers of teaching materials and training for counseling and student-support professionals. NCYI helps meet the immediate needs of students throughout the nation by ensuring those who mentor them are well prepared to respond across the developmental spectrum.

Connect With Us Online!

@nationalcenterforyouthissues

@ncyi

@nationalcenterforyouthissues